Why Some Animals Eat Their Young

A SURVIVOR'S GUIDE
TO MOTHERHOOD

Dallas Louis

SANDRA JONAS
PUBLISHING

Sandra Jonas Publishing
PO Box 20892
Boulder, CO 80308
www.sandrajonaspublishing.com

Printed in the United States of America
27 26 25 24 23   3 4 5 6 7 8

Book design: Sandra Jonas
Cover art: Adobe Stock/Rogistok
Cover design: Caeli Smith and Sandra Jonas

Publisher's Cataloging-in-Publication Data

Names: Louis, Dallas, author.
Title: Why Some Animals Eat Their Young: A Survivor's Guide to
    Motherhood / Dallas Louis.
Description: Boulder, CO : Sandra Jonas Publishing, 2021.
Identifiers: LCCN 2021933176 | ISBN 9781954861954 (hardcover) |
    ISBN 9781954861947 (ebook) | ISBN 9781954861930
    (paperback)
Subjects: LCSH: Louis, Dallas. | Motherhood—Humor. | Parenting—
    Humor. | Motherhood—Anecdotes. | Parenting—Anecdotes. |
    LCGFT: Humor. | Anecdotes. | BISAC: HUMOR / Topic /
    Marriage & Family.
Classification: LCC HQ759 .L6857| DDC 306.87430207 — dc23
LC record available at http://lccn.loc.gov/ 2021933176

All photographs courtesy of the author.

To my husband, Jeff, and our three kids,
Ethan, Emma, and Elliott.
Without y'all, none of this crazy book
would have been possible.

Contents

Author's Note

These are true stories about my family. While I spill the tea on our kids' top performances, I have changed the names of some people to protect their privacy. The information and advice I offer should not be used for diagnosis or treatment or as a substitute for professional care.

1.

Get a Puppy

Our old vacuum cleaner was acting up more and more as of late, so I decided to go hunting for a new one. I had two dogs: a big, fluffy, shed-all-the-time golden retriever named Charley and a small, curly-haired, I-think-I'm-a-big-dog miniature dachshund named Faith. The dogs alone provided ample fodder for a vacuum to gobble up, but my three children were actually the most devastating for the brush and fan belt.

Infomercials, especially the ones late at night, can make you believe that this brand of machine is, in fact, the only one that can rid your home of all traces of dust, allergens, and mites that might be contemplating building a tiny city within crevices of your new-age shag carpeting—all the while holding a ten-pound cinder-block with its awesome suction power! This vacuum can do it all! Well, late at night, or actually at four in the morning, it sounded amazing. So I bought it.

Once I got it home and began using it, I was impressed—disgusted, but impressed. I was surprised that my Charley-Girl had any fur left on her body, judging from the sheer amount of it that collected in the canister of my completely sealed and allergen-contained canister. Gag.

To be honest, I fully expected the dog hair. In a house with two dogs, in Houston, Texas, there will be shedding. My shock-and-awe moment came when I moved to the couch.

After adding the wand to the end of the nozzle, I started to fish in between the cushions. I was, of course, met with immediate resistance. My first treasure was a black sock that belonged to my fourteen-year-old. Then came the delightful sounds of coins sucking their way from the bowels of the sofa through the winding hose until they finally ended up in the cyclonic tumbler, where their raucous clanking assaulted the ears of everyone in the house.

I retrieved four more socks (none of them matching), two tissues, five rubber bands, three bobby pins, one Q-tip, one string-cheese wrapper, one ballpoint pen, enough Charley hair to knit a sweater, an iPhone charger (not the wire—the plug part), and a partridge in a pear tree. The final change count was eighty-one cents—in small coins.

By the time I finished, an audience had gathered. Charley had deemed this activity "playtime" and was happily chasing the vacuum cord and the hose. She wasn't afraid of the horrific sounds emanating from this demon machine, but the cranking of the Suburban in the garage sent this sixty-five-pound dog diving for the shelter beneath my bed. (She didn't fit.)

All three of my children (plus Faith, who, incidentally, is afraid of the vacuum) had lined the stairs, their sweet little faces looking at me through the spindles on the railing as though they had never seen anything like this before. Meanwhile, I was sweating like I had just run a marathon. One of them said, "Mom, what in the world are you doing?"

I tried to speak, but no words came out. The concept of chores had somehow, somewhere along the way, been lost on my pampered offspring. Here I was slaving, sucking up their socks, their rubber bands, their trash, and a whopping eighty-one cents when a thought occurred to me . . .

I know why some animals eat their young.

A few years ago, I ran away from home. I realize that I might be a tad too old to officially play that card, but due to circumstances totally outside my control, it was unavoidable. You see, I had lost a battle with my children—I knew it would happen one day. But the war was far from over.

Every good general needs some time to regroup for her next plan of attack. It was during my regrouping phase that my husband, Jeff, sensed that the children were mounting a substantial rebellion. So he packed me up and sent me to California to visit my parents and sisters.

What caused such a dramatic exit from my life?

A plastic cup. Yes, you read that correctly. A plastic cup. My eight-year-old daughter, Emma, had left her cup from dinner on the table overnight. This wasn't just any plastic cup. This pink speckled cup, along with its matching blue twin brothers, had been in our house for years. They were microwave and dishwasher safe. They were sandbox safe. They were puppy safe. I am almost certain at least one or all had been run over by the lawn mower and my truck. Still safe! Until that morning.

I'm a very early riser. I prefer a 4 a.m. wake-up call because that's the only time of day my house is quiet and peaceful. On this particular morning, as I made my way rather sleepily (no one pops out of bed wide awake) to the back door to let out the dog, I stepped barefooted in something wet, and my eyes flew open.

Somehow in the night, this seemingly indestructible pink cup had mysteriously split in two places down *both* sides—by itself—

and the remains of my daughter's dinner milk was everywhere. It was in the grooves of my wooden table, in the chair cushion, under the table, and as an added bonus—having used the grout of my kitchen tile as some sort of a super highway, traveling distances I would have deemed impossible for milk to travel—it was all over the floor.

But why was the cup still sitting on the kitchen table overnight?

Well, Emma was very headstrong and believed things should be handled in a certain way. According to her, everyone in the house had to wait on her—her brothers, her parents (not going to happen), and any grandparent or friend who might be unlucky enough to enter our home. Emma is in the middle of two brothers, and she suffered terribly from a disorder I have named Princess Syndrome. She developed it at a very young age.

One of the symptoms of this disorder was her refusal to clear her plate after meals. She claimed to "forget" and would leave the table and all her items behind. Jeff and I decided to try a little experiment to see how long and how many dishes could accumulate at her place before she stopped "forgetting" and resumed normal and responsible behavior. But our brilliant plan backfired. At four-thirty in the morning of the first day, I found myself on my hands and knees mopping up curdled milk from the night before.

Emma had won round one, and she didn't even know it!

Throughout this book, I will introduce you to most of the members of my family, from the obvious (husband and kids) to the obscure (in-laws, out-laws), along with numerous friends and acquaintances. Right now, though, I'll just cover the basics: My husband and I have three children. In fact, we (and when I say "we," I really mean "I") had those children in twenty-six months. Let that sink in for a minute: Three kids, twenty-six-months, no multiple births. Let me warn you: This isn't good for your body or your mind. Both will come out slightly worse for wear by the time all is said and done.

Please do not misunderstand me. I love my children! I wouldn't trade them for anything—well, except that one time, during that one week, when I traded everything and everyone for a plane ticket, some airline peanuts, and some much-needed rest and relaxation that landed me in sunny San Diego with my sisters.

Since this book is about my young'uns, I suppose we should start with how they arrived. Parenthood can be planned. In many various and creative ways, you can decide when, where, and how to become a parent. In today's society, there's a virtual cornucopia of paths to choose from.

Option Number One: Distance yourself from any and all traditional forms of birth control (pills, IUDs, condoms) and just let nature take its course.

Option Number Two: Buy books to assist with your education on charting body temperature that include graphs for charting said body temperatures and instructions on how to interpret those charts. This option requires a bit more planning on your part. In my humble opinion, this option is exhausting, but eventually it should get the job done.

Option Number Three: See a doctor. I know there are some sisters out there reading this book who wish getting pregnant were as easy as charting body temperature. I get that. I understand, and I am not minimizing the struggle many parents-to-be deal with on a daily basis. My job is to add humor to where there may have been a vacancy.

Option Number Four: Catalogs. Well, maybe not this year's Amazon's annual Prime Day Sneak Peek, but Option Number Four is the most intentional means of planning to parent in the world: adoption. Some women actually do wake up six months pregnant. I never did, but I hear it can happen. I have *never* heard of someone waking up halfway through an adoption. Adoption doesn't sneak up on you. It's a process that can take years and thousands of dollars, but in the end, you have a child you all but handpicked.

Through every step and phase of these various forms of acquiring our babies, we read books, talk to people who have survived it, and, of course, watch TV. We build up in our minds the way we think having and raising babies is supposed to happen. We do this with the hope of trying to better prepare ourselves for the task at hand: What in the world are we going to do with these perfect little angels once we invite them into our hearts and bring them into our homes? Having lived through this initial stage of preparation three times, might I make a suggestion to any first-time trying-to-be mommies out there?

Get a puppy.

Puppies are cute, require a fair amount of attention, and give you unconditional love. Best of all, you don't have to birth them. If you get a puppy and still want a baby, read on. That's what happened to me.

You see, I wanted to be a mother from a young age. In fact, it was all I ever really wanted to be when I grew up. I dabbled with thoughts of becoming a teacher or a nurse, but the nurse thing went out the door as soon as I realized I faint dead away at the sight, mention, or mere thought of blood or bodily fluids. And teachers are probably the most underappreciated people on the face of the planet.

So I reverted back to my original plan: marry the man of my dreams and raise the picture-perfect family you find on TV, in the movies, or on the cover of magazines of *Good Housekeeping* and

Family Circle. Had I known twenty years ago just how closely my family would actually resemble a *circus*, not a circle, perhaps I would have given more thought to the nursing school idea!

I'm the oldest of four girls. There's a considerable age gap between my sisters and me, which gave me the opportunity to "play house" with them and actually use real babies. I dressed them up. I fed them. I even changed diapers. Lots and lots of diapers. I may have allowed one or two of them to roll off of my bed just once or twice (Sorry, Mother. Now you know what's wrong with those two!). I was a built-in babysitter for my parents.

But there's one big difference between babysitting someone else's children and rearing your own: I could always hand my sisters *back* to my mother when they proved to be too much of a handful for me. When caring for your own kiddos, you are always IT. There's no second-string quarterback. I must admit that thought didn't fully sink in until the hospital sent me home with my first child. By then it was much too late to change my mind.

This book is about how I survived after acting upon those basic urges to procreate. I'll share highlights of what happened in my world once Jeff and I brought home three kids in a time span that was barely long enough to build a house, let alone build three humans. I pray you find comfort in knowing that you aren't the only one suffering from post-traumatic stress disorder or buyer's remorse. And, yes, it's okay to admit that both of those conditions apply to parenting, although hopefully not all the time.

I want to help you survive your own parenting journey, especially while your kids are little. Thankfully, my children have outgrown some of the antics found nestled within these pages. They still do plenty of things to keep me on my toes, but at least I get to sleep through the night, and I don't change diapers anymore.

Parenting is truly one of the most rewarding experiences of

your life, and when done right, it will also be one of the most heartbreaking. Our children need us to be more than friends, more than fun, more than cool. They need us to be their parents.

So please, sit back, grab a cup o' joe, and enjoy the trials and tribulations racing through my mind as I offer you a bit of hope and encouragement—with some humor mixed in for good measure.

2.

Dazed and Diapered

Jeff and I had been married about six months when I was bitten by the baby bug. I announced to him one evening that I thought we needed "to start trying." In all his male wisdom, he blankly stared back at me over his dinner plate and asked, "Trying to do what?" Duh.

I explained that I was ready to have a baby and asked him for his thoughts on procreation. He didn't really have much to say except that he knew what was involved in getting the little bundles of joy here, and needless to say, he fully committed to the process of "trying."

We had no idea what we had just done. At the time this conversation was taking place, every single couple we knew was having trouble getting pregnant. Every. Single. One. I have to wonder if they were doing something wrong. It took us two months. I think we needed that second month only because we started trying near the end of my cycle. Turns out, *getting* me pregnant wasn't going to be the issue: *Not keeping* me pregnant was going to be the bigger challenge.

When we saw two pink lines on the first home pregnancy test, I immediately bought every parenting and pregnancy book known to mankind. I was going to fully educate myself on the mysteries taking place inside my body. Oh sure, I had taken biology in high school, but suddenly that seemed like a really, really long time ago.

Unfortunately, those books didn't help much. In fact, they really didn't do much except scare the life out of me with all their warnings and horror stories about the 0.00002456 percent chance that my baby was going to be born her own sister because I had eaten sushi the week before I knew I was pregnant. Couple that with all the medication I was taking to ward off the extreme nausea, and—voilà!—he was also going to be armless and legless if he managed to arrive at all!

I also bought my loving husband books on how to love your wife through her pregnancy, how to be a first-time daddy, and, of course, every first-time parent's bible: *What to Expect When You're Expecting* and *What to Expect the First Year.* I'm not sure Jeff ever opened those books, and I only skimmed them. I used them mainly as doorstops to hold open my front and back doors on those rare days in Houston when the humidity was low and temperatures cooperated. Books as big as those are quite capable of preventing doors from slamming shut!

I found out quickly that not all men find the miracle of growing a human life inside of you, well, all that miraculous. I also discovered that "the glow" you hear about is nothing more than the sweat that glistens on your forehead after you have vomited for the forty-second time that day. For the record, I had that glow for twenty-six months straight. You could have used me as a night-light.

When I got pregnant with my first child, I was thrilled. Overwhelmed, but thrilled. When you're pregnant with baby number one, you have the freedom to envision how grand your life is going to be. Moreover, you have delusions—I mean, visions—of the millions of things you are *not* going to do with your child. You keep a running mental tally of the scores of mistakes your friends are making with their little spawns, and you know full well that you can do better. Your child will *not* act like that in public! You will *not* offer a bribe to your child in lieu of proper discipline. Let's face it: with a baby in the belly and none to chase at home, life is good. Hormones make you hallucinate. When you are pregnant with numero uno, you have the time to obsess over how perfect little junior will be as he effortlessly pops out into the world and you lovingly gaze into the eyes of your adoring spouse—while your pre-pregnancy jeans wait for you in your pre-packed hospital bag.

Two words: Dream on.

I am here to tell you all the things your friends won't and the things the other books are too afraid to print. Your favorite soap opera lies to you. All of those wonderfully beautiful women with perfectly round baby bumps? Very seldom does that happen in real life. Those women (a) aren't actually pregnant, (b) have spent hours in hair and makeup because ratings would significantly drop if the producers put an actual pregnant woman on the air with the real pregnancy "glow," and (c) stay "pregnant" for eighteen months with their brother's baby and then deliver a preemie.

Coming back to reality: Your boobs will swell to the size of county fair watermelons while you're pregnant. I am not even kidding. Your husband will think he has died and gone to motorboat heaven—until he discovers that he can't touch them because anything that swells that much that fast will hurt. After delivery, you may as well call *The Guinness Book of World Records*. With my first baby, Ethan, I went from a pre-pregnancy B cup to an after-baby EE cup.

I thought Jeff's eyes were going to pop out of his head. I couldn't walk upright without a cane.

These days hospitals will keep you only long enough to ensure that you get the right kid from the nursery. Even with all the experience I had growing up, I was terrified to be sent home with our firstborn and nothing more than my dear husband for support. The nurses assured me that Jeff and I were smart and capable and could handle this.

Three days later, I proved them wrong. I mentioned earlier that I grew up with sisters. God has a wonderful sense of humor, making my first child a boy. As you may know, boys come packaged a bit differently than girls. In fact, boys come packaged a lot differently than girls: They have an extra appendage. These extra appendages require extra care.

We had Ethan circumcised by our pediatrician in the hospital before we were released. She came in and informed us (very matter-of-factly) of the care and cleaning we would need to perform once we took our sweet baby home. I got very light-headed. Jeff got very pale. Apparently neither one of us would have made good nurses.

To keep the circumcision nice, neat, and tidy, Ethan's doctor placed a ring around the tip of his penis. Over the next few days this ring would fall off. We just needed to keep it clean. Sounds easy, right? Wrong.

I blame it all on sleep—or lack thereof. You see, babies don't sleep. Well, they probably sleep more than their parents. Correction: They sleep more than their *mothers*. Babies are incredibly noisy sleepers. They make all sorts of grunts and groans that lead new mothers to believe that they are hungry, wet, or at the very least awake and must be tended to right away.

Hear me when I tell you this: They are awake when they cry, not before. As a new mother, I didn't know the difference between a grunt and a hungry cry. I hadn't slept in a week. I now had sandpaper on the inside of my eyelids every time I tried to blink or close my eyes. That, dear friends, is an awesome sensation. When

Ethan was hovering somewhere around a week old, he made a noise, so I got up. I changed his diaper and nursed him from one side. (Side note on breast feeding: In the beginning, nursing feels as though you have smashed your breast through a meat grinder permanently stuck on the slowest possible speed with the dullest possible blade.) I prepared to change his diaper again. Every time this kid nursed, he pooped. I was crying.

Ethan hated having his diaper changed. He *hated* it. I can't explain why. Perhaps it was the cold air on his baby bum. Or it was the shock of being undressed. Maybe he just didn't like me to put him down. Who knows! He would cry. He would scream. He would kick. He would pee all over me.

On this particular night, my reflexes weren't as fast as they had been on previous nights. As he kicked, his heel caught the edge of the diaper, hooking the inside edge of the circumcision ring and pulling it halfway off. I screamed. Ethan screamed. Jeff, who up to this point had been peacefully sleeping five feet from all of this activity, almost had a heart attack.

Here's the deal: Every night since we brought Ethan home, Jeff had slept through all the feedings, diaper changes, and breathing checks only to greet me each morning with un-circled eyes and a smile. "How'd the baby do last night?"

But this was one night he couldn't ignore. I was hysterical. Ethan was peeing all over the place. I was screaming, "I broke him! I broke him!"

Jeff was delirious—I had awakened him from a dead sleep. That amazes me, even now, twenty years later. We had to take off the ring. Well, Jeff had to take off the ring. I couldn't do it. It was awful. He manned up and did it.

Ethan survived. Amazingly enough, all was still intact. I nursed him back to sleep, and we made it through the night. Funny thing, though, I didn't sleep for another three years.

Sleep is overrated.

I prayed for a girl the next time around.

I was thankful that Ethan was a record-holding nurser. The kid could feed! I was never really one of those mothers who follow all the "experts" about only feeding every two hours or four hours or whatever the latest and greatest rule on the street said. I'm not so sure any of those so-called experts have ever held a baby, let alone have had children of their own.

I didn't know exactly how much milk Ethan was getting. I didn't have hash marks on my breasts measured out in ounces— although some strategically placed stretch marks would have helped! The bottom line was this: Whenever he seemed hungry, I fed him. I found out that I could do a lot of things with one hand that I previously thought required two. I could eat with one hand. I could make a bed with one hand. If the need was really great, I could go to the bathroom while nursing a baby.

This kid *loved* to eat! I was his favorite meal ticket and pacifier rolled into one. That made it all the more strange when he quit nursing cold turkey at about five months old. I wasn't sure what to make of it. He was growing. He was healthy. He was eyeing the mashed potatoes around the dinner table, so maybe he was just hungry and wanted people food.

I was disappointed that he didn't want to nurse anymore. I'd had plans for our first baby. Big plans. His little life was all laid out. I was going to nurse him for a year (or so I thought). That was what was best for him. Everyone said so. And I really enjoyed breast-feeding—well, once I got over the first couple of weeks of sheer agony. I loved the bonding time, the cuddle time. It was special.

About six weeks after Ethan decided he was done nursing, it dawned on me that Aunt Flo hadn't paid me any visits. I wasn't too concerned. Perhaps my system needed a bit more time to adjust.

Two weeks later and still no impending visit from my aunt, I called my doctor. He advised me to take a pregnancy test. Why? I had just had a baby and just finished nursing that baby. There was *no way* I could possibly be pregnant.

I was wrong.

Apparently, using breastfeeding as a form of reliable birth control is an old wives' tale. You absolutely can conceive while nursing. Here's the kicker: Ethan knew it before I did. The influx of hormones into my system due to the conception of his impending little sister changed the flavor of his food supply. That's why he quit nursing cold turkey. He didn't like the taste of the milk anymore.

So we were going to have another baby. Super. They were going to be close. Really close. Really, *really* close. Ethan would turn one in August, and Baby Number Two would arrive in October. You do the math.

When Jeff and I celebrated our first wedding anniversary, I was pregnant with Ethan. When we celebrated our second anniversary, I was pregnant with Emma. I just hadn't figured it out yet. Having only dated for seven months before we got married, I realized that at this point, Jeff had known me longer pregnant than not pregnant.

Thankfully, he doesn't spook easily. I wasn't what most people would call a "peach" while pregnant. I didn't throw knives or spit fire, but my body simply didn't handle the whole thing very well. I could get pregnant, no problem there. I was just among some of the sickest folks on the planet while I was cooking those little honey buns. The sicker I got, the more dehydrated I got; the more dehydrated I got, the more often I had to make a run to the hospital for fluids. Fantastic. That cycle bumped me right up into the "high risk" category. Remember "the glow"? I had that eerie shimmer all the stinking time.

Jeff and I didn't have any family nearby during the first year and a half of our marriage. That made it harder for me to deal with the challenges of a difficult pregnancy with Emma while trying to chase down an active infant. My parents lived in Austin during this time (a solid two-and-a-half-hour drive from us) and were busy with their two restaurants and my three little sisters, who were still in middle school and high school.

All my in-laws lived out of state, including my mother-in-law, Carol. Her permanent address with the post office listed a home just south of Chicago, Illinois. But after the birth of her first grandbaby, her heart found it more and more troublesome to stay out of Texas. She kept American Airlines in business during his first year as she flew back and forth once a month to check up on him.

It was during one of her routine visits to Houston that I learned the difference between false labor and the real deal. I was stuck in Houston traffic on the way to the airport to pick up Carol when I started having Braxon Hicks contractions (false labor), or at least that's what I thought. I'd had my fair share of them with Ethan, so I wasn't concerned about experiencing some of the same with Emma.

Being stuck on Beltway 8 was actually a blessing because I had the chance to time the contractions. When I noticed my contractions' regularity, they were ten minutes apart. Sweet. Houston traffic was an excellent place to go into preterm labor. If I had to deliver this baby in my truck, she could have easily been in middle school before the traffic jam cleared out. This was not exactly ideal. I called my doctor. I told him I was going to grab my mother-in-law from passenger pickup and we would meet him at the hospital.

No big deal, right?

By the time traffic started moving and I picked up Carol, my contractions were six minutes apart and getting stronger—and I was getting nervous. I should get extra bonus points for nearly making my mother-in-law faint. I told her I couldn't help her with her bags because I was in labor and we really needed to hurry. Honestly, I thought she was a goner!

We called Jeff on our way to labor and delivery. He was en route from a business meeting two hours away and quite possibly breaking land speed records to get to me. Once we made it to the hospital, I did have enough sense to pull right up to the door and let Carol go park my SUV. Why I was still driving is beyond me. Maybe I have control issues . . .

Contractions: Five minutes and counting. Time to panic.

It was too early for this baby to come. Six and a half months is not a prime delivery date.

Three minutes, two and a half centimeters dilated. Immediately the nurses inserted an IV, and the medication started flowing. My heart rate sped up and the contractions stopped. This baby girl (shrouded in drama) was trying very hard to make her appearance early.

My doctor was furious with me. Dr. Wilson is the most kind and understanding man to go through pregnancies with. But on that day, "kind and understanding" didn't come to mind.

"You already weren't feeling well? You *still* went to the airport? You *waited* to come here? Bed rest."

He may have well just broken my legs. I hate being still. I hate being told to be still. What was worse, I had a witness. Carol was standing right beside my bed, promising to be my warden while she was in town. She stayed an extra week.

Turns out, Emma was a smidgen impatient. She wanted to do things her way. She still does. She ended up staying put until fairly close to her due date (about three weeks prior to), although looking back, delivering early was probably my fault.

Note to self: Do not ingest castor oil unless you feel like inducing hard labor and are prepared to play catch with your newborn. I had heard that castor oil could possibly bring on labor. I had no idea how fast it would work. In my defense, I was sort of done being pregnant. If you think about it, I had been pregnant for a couple of years by this point.

So start to finish, Emma was born in two and half hours. That is from the very first contraction to the final push. Jeff was super excited. He had always wanted to drive to the hospital like Mario Andretti! I, on the other hand, was concerned that he might have to morph from Mario to McSteamy if he had to deliver his daughter in the front seat of my truck.

Might I take this opportunity to make another public service announcement? To those of you contemplating a more natural birth plan, pass on it. Take the drugs. I had two kids with drugs, one without. Take the drugs as soon as they're offered. Your anesthesiologist will become your best friend. You will love him more and more with every push of that magic little button. Trust me on this one. Needless to say, with Emma, no drugs.

Delivering a baby with no medication is the weirdest feeling in the world. It is not magical. It is not enlightening. It didn't make me more of a real woman. I simply didn't have time to get an epidural. But I did feel better *after* delivery. I could get up and walk around. I could feel my legs. That was nice. But I can't lie to you, the during part was rough.

Dazed and diapered. That was us. I had two itty-bitty ones at home. They were happy and healthy—a matched set, a boy and a girl. Life was good and we were done. Carol was still visiting, longer this time than usual, but I was grateful. I needed the extra help.

Jeff was becoming a hands-on dad. He wasn't as afraid to pick up this second baby as he was the first. Whenever Ethan would cry as a newborn, Jeff would hold him at arm's length as though the kid were a bomb and might explode at any given moment. He had come to realize that babies cry and rarely do they explode.

So holding them close to your body was not only a safe bet but also a good call, because in most cases, it would quiet their cries.

We were also talking about him going to see that "special" doctor. We (I) had all we could handle with these two babies. We didn't need any more. We were doing all right. Or so we thought . . .

There comes a pivotal moment in everyone's life where you have an opportunity to make a choice. I will forever remember our moment.

When Emma was barely six weeks old, Jeff was packing up to head out for a weeklong business trip. He traveled a lot for work then, often being gone anywhere from four to six days a week, two to three weeks a month. It was hectic around the house when he wasn't home.

His mother was still visiting and she had taken the kids on an outing, so the two of us were alone. It was rare that our house was empty. Well, as we said our goodbyes, one thing led to another, and a quick kiss goodbye turned into a long kiss goodbye, and fifteen minutes later, he went away for his weeklong trip feeling very satisfied. I went through the rest of my day with a bit more spring in my step as well.

Life returned to normal. Jeff's mother told us she was moving in. Ethan was adjusting to Emma. Emma was adjusting to life on the outside. I was adjusting to life with two babies. Jeff made his appointment with the special doctor.

Then Emma quit nursing.

I almost fainted.

I couldn't bring myself to go to the store and buy the test. I had to call in reinforcements. I rang up my friend Ann. She popped over with a two-pack test kit, plus a bonus stick. I took one immediately. Positive. I drank half a gallon of apple juice and took the second test. *More* positive.

I sat down in the middle of my bathroom floor and cried.

I waited until the next morning to take the third and final test. Super positive. I always was a test-taking overachiever. I had to tell my husband. I mean, I seriously could not keep this from him. Incidentally, it happened to be the morning of his special appointment. I laid all three tests on the bathroom counter. He turned white as a ghost and dropped into my chair that I normally sit in to put on my makeup. He sat there for ten solid minutes. He would look at me, then look at the tests, and then back at me. He just shook his head.

Jeff had gotten used to going to the doctor with me. He would watch as I quietly went through the mortification of disrobing, trying to cover myself with something slightly smaller than an oversized BBQ napkin, and then climbed onto a frigid metal table and waited (an eternity) for the doctor to make his way into the room.

But Jeff's appointment was a completely different story. This man mumbled and groaned and complained and mumbled some more with every single piece of clothing he took off.

He unhooked his belt: "This is ridiculous."

He untucked his shirt: "It's cold in here."

He unbuttoned his pants: "Are you"—looking at me—"going to watch?"

He muttered something colorful when he discovered he had forgotten to remove his shoes before trying to remove his pants.

He climbed onto the table and tried (unsuccessfully) to position his very own teeny-tiny BBQ napkin to effectively cover himself: "This stupid thing is too small! It doesn't fit."

He fidgeted: "How long do I have to sit here—"

In walked the doctor.

Dr. Snippet: "Good morning, Mr. Louis. How are you this morning?"

Jeff: "Fine."

Dr. Snippet: "That's great." He looked at his chart. "I see we're here today for a vasectomy. Are you sure?" The doctor looked at me.

Jeff (through gritted teeth and no smile): "Pretty sure. She told me this morning that's she's pregnant—again."

Dr. Snippet: "Wonderful! Congratulations! How many will this make?"

Me: "This is number three. Our son is one, and our daughter is eight weeks old. Please do a good job."

Dr. Snippet: "Wow. Let's get started then. Now, Mr. Louis, if you could just lie back and put your feet in the stirrups so I can have a look . . ."

I smiled. I know it's mean and a bit deranged, but I seriously could have probably died happy right then and there. For years I listened to Jeff tell me there was nothing to this doctor thing. Nothing? Not until the stirrup is on the other foot.

After his little visit, he had a whole new appreciation for what I went through at my appointments. But please don't feel too bad for him: he survived his ordeal in a much better state than I was surviving mine.

Baby number three was proving to be a much bigger problem than babies one and two combined. I'm not a very big person. My driver's license says I stand in at five foot three inches. That sounds about right if I have on my big-girl shoes. Flat-footed, I'm not so sure. I didn't weigh much more a hundred pounds even with all the heavily magnified boob weight I was toting around.

So you can imagine everyone's alarm when it wasn't simply fluid I was losing but actual pounds. I lost fifteen pounds before I was halfway through my first trimester, which, needless to say, landed me back at the hospital. Good ol' Dr. Wilson was more than peeved that I had wound up pregnant so soon again and was determined to see a healthy mom and a healthy baby all the way to full term. So rather than pumping me with fluid and sending me home, he kept me—my bouts of champion nausea bought me several weeks of vacation at a happening little hotspot known as St. Luke's Medical Center on the North Side.

If Elliott (gift number three) had been my first baby, he would be an only child. You can take that to the bank.

On top of that were the crazy-making hormones. Hormones cause a woman to behave in mannerisms outside the patterns of normal society. But when that same woman is pregnant—watch out and hide the ammunition! She now has a chemical world war raging inside her body that she has absolutely no control over.

Every time (there were more than a couple) I found myself stranded in a hospital room, it was for no less than one week. This made parenting the two babies left at home exceedingly difficult. I'm thankful my mother-in-law was there to pick up the slack that I couldn't even look at, let alone carry.

Jeff was struggling too. He was still traveling for work several days a week, and when he was home, he needed to be in the office. Having a wife confined to a hospital bed in the farthest reaches of the city was more than a bit inconvenient.

My "vacation" added a large dose of stress to our marriage. Let me tell you something, girls, it's perfectly okay to be frustrated with your husband. Jeff was plenty frustrated with me, although I'm not sure how I could have changed my end of the situation. I was hooked up to several different monitors and machines to track my heart rate and the baby's. My blood pressure needed constant monitoring because it was very low. I was on numerous IV fluids, so walking around was a complete pain and leaving the hospital a near impossibility. Therefore, Jeff had to come to me.

Have you ever been in a situation where you knew it would be better if you could just remain quiet? I vaguely remembered something my grandmother told me a long time ago: "Dallas, if you can't say anything nice, then don't say anything at all." I could have heeded those pearls of wisdom, but instead of walking in the light, I chose a much darker, more sinister path. I allowed the stir-craziness that had been building up inside me to spew out, and two highly stressed individuals collided in a hospital room on the maternity floor one night.

Here's the rundown: Jeff had come for a visit. Although, truth be told, on this particular evening, it felt more like a "I have to be here because you are my wife" type of visit. At any rate, I wasn't thrilled to see him nor was he jumping for joy over being there. Both of us said some things that shouldn't have been said, and the floor nurses enjoyed front-row seats to the scene.

In retrospect, "scene" may not actually or adequately capture the essence of the energy that went down between us. It was more like a Broadway extravaganza or Hollywood blockbuster in brilliant Technicolor. I ended up telling him that I didn't need or want his sympathy, and furthermore, if this was the way he was going to behave, he could just stay away.

He didn't say another word. He simply turned and walked out. The door closed smartly behind him. I was completely numb. Every marriage, every relationship, goes through something similar. Daily stress will get the better of you, and words will get said that should have stayed circling the drain of your mental filter. Jeff was under a tremendous amount of stress. He was dealing with being both Mommy *and* Daddy, running a business located in two different Texas cities, making sure his mother was taken care of (remember she was living with us), and worrying about me and the baby I was carrying.

That's a terribly heavy load for one man to lug around on his shoulders. In my own defense, I couldn't attend to those two babies at home because every time I took more than two steps, I threw up. I was exhausted, dehydrated, and starving. I had been stuck in this same hospital bed for longer than I cared to remember, and if my doctor didn't do something brilliant, I would remain in it until I delivered this baby!

Mix all this stress with some high-grade hormonal weapons of mass destruction and you have an explosion of astronomical proportions just waiting to happen. Jeff and I were having a hard time remembering how I got pregnant in the first place.

As it happens, my doctor did do something brilliant. He installed a diabetic pump into my leg. No, I didn't develop gestational diabetes. But this little miracle pump could administer my nausea medication on the same schedule as it would for a diabetic needing insulin. In short, this was my ticket out of Hotel St. Luke. The pump shot meds into my leg every seven minutes, bringing me enough time to play with my babies. It didn't fix me completely, but it helped.

My living room was much closer than my hospital room at St. Luke's. Jeff and I made up as well. We realized that our tensions were running high and our emotions were stretched super thin. Getting married isn't the hardest thing you will ever need to adjust to in life—it's throwing kids into that mix. Aside from being sicker than a dog for the entire nine months of my pregnancy with Elliott, I delivered an extremely healthy, seven-pound baby boy (only three weeks early). This child has a plan and a purpose. He is my walking, talking miracle.

Through the sleep-deprived fog that enveloped my brain, I remembered the whole circumcision ring debacle, so I was much more careful this time around. Elliott survived the first two weeks of his life with almost no mishaps. Almost. We did bring him home to a one-year-old (only by eight days) sister and a two-year-old (by three months) brother. Their idea of a family welcome gift? Emma threw the television remote at him and knocked him square in the head. Apparently, she wanted a sister. I assured her that I couldn't return him. She still stands by that request today and remains miffed.

During the early weeks following Elliott's arrival, I began to feel overwhelmed. I know what you're thinking: *Now* she feels overwhelmed? You see, my mother-in-law had decided that since Houston was going to be her new permanent residence, a job should be the next step in her assimilation process. Jeff was still traveling for most of the week, which translated to most of the month. So I was at home alone with three small children—actually at home alone with three small babies.

Elliott decided that screaming was much better and more effective than mere crying. For the record, there is a substantial difference between a crying baby and a screaming baby. The only thing that came close to quieting the cries emanating from his tiny body was using me as a pacifier. One morning, I had just positioned myself on the couch, took a deep and (unsuccessful) calming breath, and shoved Elliott's favorite "binky" into his mouth when I heard glass shattering in the kitchen.

Kids are so smart, especially in their natural habitat. Can we take a moment to appreciate their cunning and creativity? Ethan and Emma knew that when I assumed the position, supported (and pinned in) by the various couch pillows needed and necessary to properly maintain my feeding stance for the baby, I was somehow out of commission when it came to reaching them in their hour of greatest mischief.

They were wrong.

I immediately and forcibly removed Elliott from me, which threw him into uncontrollable fits of hysteria, and vaulted over the back of the couch, only to find Ethan and Emma *standing* on top of the kitchen table staring down at the shattered pieces of a red vase that held the remains of flowers, which should have been thrown out long ago.

The timeline of tossing out flowers wasn't how I chose to focus my attention, but rather, I directed my line of fire at my two-year-old, all the while perfecting my Spider Man skills by jumping from chair to barstool to chair. "Don't move!" I screamed. "Stay where you are! Ethan, what did you do? Why did you let your sister onto the table?"

Pause.

Does anyone else see something wrong with those questions? For starters, Ethan was two. He was behaving like a normal two-year-old. Normal two-year-olds climb on top of tables, dragging their one-year-old little sister with them, and occasionally break vases.

His mother, by contrast, was behaving like a wild lunatic. This impromptu role-play of some twisted version of King of the Mountain was taking place to the ear-splitting serenades of a wailing infant. The look of confusion on Ethan's face should have been a clue to me—but rational thought had left the building, and Monster Mom was there in full force.

She was still ranting, still charging, still grappling over furniture and dangling over broken glass, fully expecting her two-year-old son to explain in a coherent manner the whys and hows behind the broken vase. Of course, that didn't happen.

I grabbed both kids in a kind of football hold and exited the kitchen via a glass-free route and banished them to the safety of the upstairs. I resumed my position on the couch and attempted to calm the screaming banshee I had left there moments earlier.

You would think that having nursed all three of my children for as long as I had, my breasts would have been totally used to the constant tug of the necessary suction from operating as a food source. Completely not true. As Ethan and Emma were upstairs crying, partially from their relief at having escaped the wrath of their fire-breathing mother and partially from their banishment to the upstairs, I sat on the couch with the baby. And both of us cried. He would suck for the count of five, release, and then cry, to which my toes would curl up to my knees, and I would cry.

This went on and on. I sat on the couch and sobbed about the mess I had somehow gotten myself tangled in. The best part: There was still glass to clean up when I was done nursing the baby. Awesome.

I somehow managed to clean up the glass without seriously injuring myself or anyone else. Elliott never stopped crying. The other two were released from the upstairs prison, but they kept a wide berth. I was a complete catastrophe. My nerves were shot. I had held Elliott *all day long*. Every time I attempted to put him down, he screamed until I thought my ears would burst.

It was late afternoon before Ethan dared to approach me for anything. I happened to be in the kitchen, so I suppose he thought it was safe to ask for a drink.

A simple petition for a cup of juice might as well have been a request for the launch sequence from NASA for a rocket to the space station. With a squirming infant in one hand and an uncooperative sippy cup in the other, I'd had all I could handle. When I finally secured the lid nice and tight, rather than handing it to my patiently waiting child, I *threw it*. Then I promptly sat down on the kitchen floor and started to cry—again. Ethan took one look at me and calmly and quietly took his little sister by the hand and led her away from me and went back upstairs. I cried even harder.

While sitting in a puddle of my own tears and self-pity, I made a phone call to a friend, who came to my rescue (and that of my kids). She packed up everybody and hauled them all over to her house to play with her kiddos for a few hours. I needed a nap. Did you know that losing one hour of sleep for six consecutive nights has the same effect on your body as pulling an all-nighter? That, dear friends, is just for one week. I had a newborn of some shape or fashion in my house for *two years.*

If a new mom loses only one hour of sleep a night, she will still be tired, but new moms lose way more than one hour. My three babies woke up at different times. With that type of sleep deprivation, coupled with the hormonal craziness going on inside me, was it any wonder that I was trying to pitch a no-hitter in my kitchen? I began to think I might need some pharmaceutical intervention.

Incidentally, that very night, I pulled Jeff out of bed around two-thirty by one of his favorite appendages just so he could sit at my feet and simply be close enough for me to reach while I nursed his baby for the forty-seventh time that day. I was tired. I was tired of being the only one who could feed the baby. I was tired of being the only one who could hear the other two cry in the night. I slept (and I use the word "slept" incredibly loosely) with *two* baby monitors on my side of the bed. I had to write the kids' names on them so I would know whose room to go to in the middle of the night fog. I was, to put it plainly, flat-out exhausted.

The next morning, I called my doctor.

He listened to me cry. He listened to me scream. He listened to me cry some more. Then he prescribed a miracle pill—an antidepressant—that made me not want to throw knives at my husband or sippy cups at the walls. I was able to adjust, breathe, and deal with having three babies at home. I found my rhythm.

Taking this little pill every day didn't mean I had failed as a mother or as a woman. No. It meant just the opposite. It meant that I recognized a problem and that I couldn't do this on my own. I also recognized that Jeff wasn't a mind reader. When I needed his help, I had to ask him.

By the way, that's still true today. I'm extremely thankful I had a friend to call when things got ugly. Parenting isn't for sissies. Those sweet little angels will test you in the most brutal ways imaginable. You will doubt everything you thought to be true about yourself—and then some.

Is it worth it?

Absolutely. Without one single, solitary doubt.

But just as you would never go camping without the proper provisions, never attempt to parent without the proper "provisions" as well. Turn to your friends, your family, your church, your neighbors for help.

I can't lie: I'm glad the extreme baby phase is over.

3.

Disney World

Have you ever planned a family vacation? Perhaps you aren't at that actual stage of parenting yet. Maybe you're still watching a lot of movies and television shows and thinking, *Gee, it sure would be nice to take a family vacation.*

My advice: Don't hurry. When our kids were little, Jeff and I thought (actually, I thought) it would be great to take them to the mother of all destinations, Walt Disney World in Orlando, Florida. Apparently I was temporarily insane. For an added bonus, we decided to make this journey over spring break, when our thirteen-year-old babysitter could go with us.

At the time of our departure from the Houston Intercontinental Airport, my children were two, three, and four years old. I'll pause for the gasp escaping from your mouth. And did I mention that my sweet husband would join us in Orlando and not fly out on the same flight? Evidently, he had a meeting of vital importance that couldn't wait. Turns out that 747s don't wait either.

So I boarded my Continental flight bound for the "happiest place on earth" with two toddlers, a preschooler, and one stunned-looking thirteen-year-old babysitter who was second-guessing her willingness to accompany me on this flying freak show.

I could feel the passengers' eyes boring into me as I passed them, each one offering up their silent prayers of *Dear God, please don't let that motley crew sit next to me.* Thankfully Florida isn't that far away from Houston. The kids did amazingly well, considering that half the time they couldn't make it through a dinner meal without wiggling uncontrollably. I burned through the battery on the portable DVD players, they ate every individual snack I packed and drank every juice box, and we went to the bathroom every thirty minutes. But through it all, they were quiet, and not one single flight attendant or sky goddess came by and offered to stow an unruly child in an overhead bin for me. I called the flight to Florida a win.

That was about to change. I have no scientific evidence to support this, but I believe that children (of any age) have only a certain number of "good points" on any given day. My kids burned every single one of them on the plane ride to Florida. They had me believing that the angelic faces they were displaying for all the world to see were actually going to be what they would exhibit for the duration of the day—or, dare I think, the rest of the trip?

Nope.

As soon as we were released from our seats and began to make our way onto the jet way, I sensed a change. Elliott was two, so he was plastered to my hip as we waited for the luggage handlers to bring his stroller up from the belly of the plane. But not Ethan and Emma. They were both unrestrained—and they both bolted.

What they failed to understand was that my babysitter, Jasmine (how fitting that she had the same name as a Disney princess), just so happened to be an all-district track star. She not only easily caught both of my runners but also managed to wrangle them back to me before I had even successfully strapped Elliott into his stroller.

With one glimpse into Ethan's eyes, I could see the wheels of his devious little mind spinning in multiple directions, planning his next escape. The walk through the jet way was slow and cumbersome. We were now burdened with overflowing diaper bags that had started out neatly packed but had been completely ransacked during the flight as I tried to keep the children quiet and calm. The two bags were currently bursting at their seams, their contents threatening to spill from the top after having been stuffed unceremoniously back into place when the wheels touched down. I'm certain I was leaving a trail of goldfish crackers mingled with Cheerios as I walked.

Halfway down the terminal, Ethan decided he no longer wanted to hold Jasmine's hand—he wanted mine. Picture this: I was pushing a monster stroller, a diaper bag hanging off each shoulder, being jostled by passengers rushing to meet their next plane or loved ones, keeping my eyes trained on my sitter (who was in charge of not losing either of the two children she had her hands on), all the while desperately trying not to mow down anyone.

Of course I could hold Ethan's squirming and sweaty hand. I could see the whole thing play out in slow motion almost before it happened. As I reached for Ethan's hand, he looked up at me with his incredible big blue eyes and his round cherub cheeks, flashed a perfectly deviously mischievous grin—and took off running.

Snap.

"Go get him," I told Jasmine. Emma stood rooted to the spot, looked up at me, laughed, and said, "Ethan fast."

Yes, I thought. *But Mommy is faster. Time for extreme measures.*

There are certain truths in life. Always wear clean underwear in case you're in an accident. Always eat your vegetables so you can grow big and strong. And my personal favorite: Never say never. It will always come back to bite you. I had so many "never's" in my vocabulary before I had children. I could write another book simply based on those!

The particular "never" that day in the airport had to do with leashes. I used to see parents with their children dragging or pulling along at the end of a leash and think to my brilliant and childless self, *What is wrong with those parents? Why can't they control their small children? When I have my own children, I will never put them on a leash!*

Well, after Ethan's second bid for freedom, I deemed it time for the puppy backpacks, aka leashes. For those of you who may not know exactly what I'm talking about, let me explain. These backpacks are soft and fluffy stuffed animals. Kids love them. They can hold them. They can love on them. They can even put a few (very few) toys into the pouch.

The backpack fits onto your child like a regular backpack and fastens across his chest so your little Houdini can't wriggle out of it. They come in several different animal varieties: puppy, monkey, frog, and one other flavor—an unknown, yet magical species. Parents love these backpacks, not because of their cuteness, but because of their six-foot-long tail.

Yes, these packs are cute and fuzzy, but can we call them what they really are? Folks, these backpacks are *leashes*.

And I bought three of them.

As Jasmine made her way back to us through the crowd with a laughing Ethan on her back, I had to regroup. I had made a big deal about how special these backpacks were and how we couldn't use them until we arrived in Florida. The kids had no idea that they were actually a restraining device. As I looked down at my firstborn, I gave him the same smile he had given me before he ran off and asked him if he was ready to put on his very special new backpack. His answer was a resounding YES! Naturally, Emma wanted hers. And Elliott followed suit. So I strapped everyone into his or her backpacks and off we went one more time, still trying to get out of the jet way.

As we finally made it down to baggage claim, I became more aware of the people in the airport. Jasmine took over care of the now-vacated stroller holding the diaper bags while I tried to corral the kids. In hindsight, I must have looked a sight! I did feel a bit like a dog walker from Central Park. I had three kids on the ends of three separate leashes, who, just like puppies on the end of their leashes, didn't know how to effectively maneuver without getting tangled up in each other's tail. We had to stop several times to untangle them. Yet we continued forward. People stopped to stare, but no one offered to help.

When we arrived at the airport in Houston to begin our adventure, Jeff had been with us. He was there for the unloading, the bagging, and the tagging of all our travel paraphernalia. But upon reaching the luggage carousel in Orlando, I found myself down one significantly strong and capable pair of hands. As I began to grab suitcase after suitcase and car seat after car seat, my mind started to really process the mountain of trouble and rubble I was quickly being buried under.

How in the wide world was I going to get all this stuff and all these kids to the rental car place? I was chanting in my head, sweat running down my back, *Please don't make us take a shuttle. Please don't make us take a shuttle.* Seven suitcases, three car seats, one stroller, all our carry-on stuff, three babies, and one sitter later, I was exhausted.

When I turned to look at the kids, they actually looked like puppies at this point. Well, puppies chasing their own tails. The newness of the backpacks had worn off, and they were trying to figure out how to get them off. They soon became convinced that the key to removing them was on their backs. So all three of them were walking in twisted circles with their little necks craned to the sides and arms up over their heads trying (without success) to reach the head of the backpack companions. I had to laugh—until I looked past them and saw the line for the rental car shuttle.

I wanted to sit on the floor and cry, but I didn't have time. After loading everything onto a trolley, I gave the kids each something they could hold to make them feel like they were helping, and away we went.

Whose idea was it to come out here? Yeah, mine. Where was my husband? He was at his meeting back in Houston, missing all the fun. Meanwhile, in Orlando, I was dealing with a wonky rental car reservation (our original one was wrong, go figure), three tired toddlers, a frustrated babysitter, and myself on the very edge of sanity.

The rental company made up for their mistake by moving us from a regular Dodge Caravan to a Grand Caravan. Typically, I'm not a fan of minivans. My preferred mode of transportation at home is something just shy of a train car on wheels. But after spending time in that mini, I could see the allure of just such a machine. It had all sorts of hidden compartments. I fit all seven suitcases in the back and behind the third seat and had room to spare while loading the kids. I was surprised that I didn't have to strap one of them to the roof.

All told, the time it took us to get our bags, go to the rental car place, load everything and everyone into the van, and get on the road was the same as the flight from Houston to Orlando.

As we drove to the resort, I couldn't help but notice the crowds. Did I mention we were in Orlando over spring break? And that Houston kids weren't the only ones out of school? There were kids everywhere. I mean All. Over. The. Place. The resort was a madhouse. It was another hour before we got settled into our condo.

But just like waiting for the minivan, the wait for our condo was more than worth it. During the unloading of the van, Jasmine kept the kids occupied while I tried to get everything in order. Right about the time I put the last suitcase into a closet, who should walk through the door? Jeff. The kids went nuts!

"Daddy!"

"We rode on a airplane!"

"I ate peanuts!"

"I watched a movie!"

"Ethan runned away from Mommy *two times*!"

Jeff looked at me and smiled.

I collapsed on the couch.

Our time at Disney World was very much like parenting. There are all sorts of things you can do while you're there that will make you laugh, cry, and want to throw up all at the same time.

One of the most obvious Disney World metaphors about parenting is the roller coaster. I personally do not handle roller coasters well. I'm nothing more than a big sissy-girl. My kids, on the other hand, aren't afraid of anything. Unfortunately for them, they have peanuts for parents, so it was a challenge finding a roller coaster that had a height requirement they could clear. We finally managed to get Ethan and Emma on Goofy's Barn Burner. Elliott was simply too much of a shrimp, which suited me just fine. The two of us stayed put safely on the ground to watch.

How many times while we're trying to parent our children do we feel as though we are actually on a roller coaster? I've often felt tossed side to side and back to front as I jostle from one parenting task to the next. Someone should have checked the height requirement on me before I decided to get pregnant with my first kiddo.

We also do a lot of waiting while we parent. We wait for our babies to arrive. We wait for them to sleep. We wait for them to talk, to grow, to walk. Most of the time we simply just stay in a state of hurry up and wait. Having visited Disney World during its absolute worst—that is, busiest—time of year, we did a lot of waiting in line.

Everywhere we went, we waited—forty-five minutes here, fifty-five minutes there—but nowhere was the line as long or as slow moving as it was for the Disney princesses.

The princesses had their own tent in a secluded section of Toon Town. I'm certain they placed them in this location to avoid disrupting the traffic flow of other park-goers. We waited in line for an hour and a half to see the princesses. I am not exaggerating.

We stood in line and counted the birds on the wall. We held our own kids and then traded with the other worn-out parents in line. We sat on the floor and held kids. We sang songs. We ate snacks. We rotated out of line to go to the bathroom. For an hour and a half we did this. All in all, I would say that the line experience was a success. By the time we managed to wend our way to the mouth of the tent, none of my children had been reduced to tears or tantrums. I was feeling like a real winner.

The staffers working the crowd gave us the initial rundown on how this little interview with the Disney royal brigade was going to play out. We would enter the tent in an orderly fashion. A total of three princesses were inside this tent, each princess partitioned off so her sister princesses were hidden from view. We were to move quickly and swiftly. Keep the line moving. Don't dawdle. The children would present their autograph books to the first princess in an orderly fashion. The parents would then take the autograph books while the children posed with the princess and then moved on to the next one. That doesn't sound too terribly difficult, does it?

Trust me when I tell you it was harder than you think.

The first princess was Sleeping Beauty. She was charming and beautiful, just as you would expect her to be. She thought Elliott was the cat's meow. She bent low over him and planted a great big kiss on his forehead. He squealed with delight. She was completely enamored of him. He was the picture of an angel, with his blond hair and the biggest and roundest blue eyes you've ever seen. His eyelashes were (and still are) the longest and blackest you've ever seen. Who would not want to just squeeze him? We had no issues with our photo session with Sleeping Beauty.

The next princess was Snow White. She, too, was just as beautiful as you could imagine. Ethan and Emma were shy about approaching her with their autograph books, but they obediently walked forward, books in hand, and posed for their picture. Elliott hung back, standing there gaping at her. She bent down to his level and, with skills only a true princess could possess, beckoned him closer with the promise of a secret. His eyes widened, and he moved closer to her. She quickly and gently cupped his chin as though she were about to whisper the secrets of her kingdom into his ear, but at the last minute and without warning, she turned his little head and planted a huge kiss on his cheek!

He screamed so loudly that everyone in the tent looked at us. My precocious two-year-old took Snow White's face in his pudgy little hands and said, "You tricked me! Can I still know your secret?"

She laughed and whispered something into his ear. He calmed down. To this day, I don't know what she said.

Now, our final princess. Ethan and Emma moved through the tent in a trancelike state that can only be attributed to being in the presence of such fantastic royalty. Elliott was skipping from cloud to cloud—having been effectively tagged by two of the world's most fabulous princesses. Both his cheek and his forehead bore the lipstick stains to prove that his time in line had not been wasted.

We knew we were about to enter the final princess room, but we didn't know which princess we'd be seeing. Disney has a ton of princesses. It could have been anyone. Tinker Bell is even considered a princess these days. Emma was the first one to catch a glimpse of our final princess. "Mommy! It's Cinderella! I can see her! Mommy! Mommy! Oh my goodness! It's Cinderella!"

And that's when Elliott lost his mind.

Up to this point, he had been content to wait his turn. He had followed the directions, moving in a swift, orderly fashion. Jeff and I had been trying to teach the boys, even at this age, to let girls go first. All our instructions flew out the window when Elliott laid eyes on his dream girl—Cinderella, who was his favorite princess and still is to this day. When he looked around that tent curtain and saw her standing there, he lost all abandon and threw his arms wide, sending his book flying. His brother and sister dived for cover as he took off in a run to greet his walking, talking, living dream come true.

Cinderella turned to look at this pint-sized bundle of love coming at her and bent low to receive the hug speeding her way. A seemingly harmless gesture, right? What poor Cindy failed to notice was that in this slow-motion run to hug that Elliott was doing, he had totally and completely dropped his left shoulder in a most impressive imitation of an NFL linebacker. So what appeared to be a sweet two-year-old was, in fact, a compact stick of dynamite love getting ready to explode all over her.

There was nothing I could do to stop it. Elliott slammed into her open arms, knocking her off her feet! She went over backward, the hoops of her dress lifting Elliott up even farther onto her chest.

Princess secret service sprang into action: "Princess down! We have a princess down!"

Emma screamed, "You BROKE HER, Elliott!"

Elliott had managed to wiggle himself up around her neck and now had her in a two-year-old headlock. Jeff and I stood rooted to the spot. We couldn't even video this debacle. Princess secret service was trying (with no avail) to get Elliott to release his grip from around Cinderella's neck. They decided it was a lost cause and picked both of them up in one fluid motion.

Elliott still hadn't let go of his dream girl. Cinderella bent down, set him gently on the ground, and pried him away from her neck. He just stood there staring into her eyes with love. Her secret service detail stood close by watching us with intense dislike.

Without missing a beat, Cinderella said "My! What a strong little prince you are!" and kissed the only remaining unkissed place left on his face: his other cheek. She posed for all the pictures with the kids, and then the secret service escorted us out.

How many times have we felt like that with our parenting? We wait and wait and wait for something, and when we finally arrive at whatever it is we've been waiting for, we simply cannot contain ourselves.

I've been there. For me, it was two pink lines. Then a very short time later, it was two more pink lines. Then (gasp!) in no time at all, two more pink lines! I wanted those babies. Then when they got here, I wanted to just *watch* them.

Granted, parenting is a whole lotta standing around with not a whole lot going on. Then other times, it was exactly like meeting Cinderella: I just couldn't contain myself.

But other times, the times we'd like to forget, it's like the Mad Tea Party ride, better known as the Spinning Teacups.

4.

Spinning Teacups

During our time at Disney, one of the rides we dared to attempt that didn't have an excruciatingly long line was the Mad Tea Party, inspired by the Mad Hatter's party in the animated classic *Alice in Wonderland*. The kids thought it would be a super-double, terrific-fun thing to do. I mean, have you seen all the teacups? My husband was cracking up at the mere thought of me climbing into one of them. I don't exactly do motion all that well. My stomach began to get very uneasy.

For those of you who haven't had the pleasure of sitting in one of these Walt Disney torture machines, here's how they work. You approach a giant, flat-surfaced area that holds many, many multicolored jumbo-sized teacups that have large steering wheels protruding up from the middle of the cup. It is all very pretty and pleasing to the eye, but then so was the field of poppies in *The Wizard of Oz*, and we all know where that landed Dorothy. Looks do not always reveal the true intent or purpose of an object.

So we all climbed aboard one of these seemingly harmless teacups (we could all fit into one) and got ready to ride around the track. It was a nice day. Kids were laughing. We could have been a commercial for Disney World. Then, without warning, the teacup began to spin rapidly on its track to the right, and my husband took the steering wheel and turned our cup to the left. We all whipped around and the kids went nuts. I could taste my lunch coming back around for a second show.

The kids were screaming, "Again! Again! More! More!" I was praying this was one of the shorter rides at the Magic Kingdom. Back and forth we went. When the cup started spinning on its track to the left, we (actually, Jeff) spun it to the right. This went on for an eternity. I understand why there was a short line at this ride. Spinning teacups: around and around you go, where you stop, nobody knows.

I told you that story so I could tell you the next one. I haven't changed the names to protect the innocent, because as this series of events unfolds, you won't find any "innocents," except maybe me. Hopefully I'll extract a modicum of pity from you.

At close to midnight one Saturday evening, my husband and I had just returned home from a rodeo fundraising gala. Hey, we live in Texas—horses, cows—it's what we do. The Houston Livestock Show and Rodeo is one of the biggest and best rodeos in the world and the pregame festivities are too good to miss. Upon arriving home, we were greeted by a very sleepy Nana (my mother-in-law, Carol).

As we said our thank-yous and goodbyes, she began looking for her shoes. Remembering that she left them outside on the table while the kids were swimming, she went to get them but found only one shoe. We knew right away that the culprit was Grace, our spunky three-and-a-half-month-old golden retriever puppy. She was going through this hide-and-seek phase. Our other dog, Littles, was much older and more "seasoned" and completely nonplussed over the arrival of Nana's shoes.

Typically, Grace didn't eat what she took. She only hid her treasures. This was *not* amusing to us at midnight. I made the comment to my mother-in-law that I hoped those weren't her favorite shoes, to which she promptly replied that yes, they were. Terrific. Jeff told her we would get her another pair, only to be told that the manufacturer no longer made this particular type. Double terrific. After thirty minutes of searching through flower beds for one brown shoe, in the dark, dressed in black-tie attire, we decided to look when we had more light. Nana put on her other shoe, limped to her vehicle, and went home, and we went to bed.

Can you feel the teacup beginning to spin?

The next morning, we didn't make it to church (perhaps that's where my day went wrong). Instead we stayed home and helped my husband pack for his business trip. Once Jeff was gone, I tried to be the fun mommy who doesn't always show up. I spend most of my days doing the less-glamorous side of motherhood, the side you don't see on daytime shows: the cooking, cleaning, laundry, carpool—the list goes on. But as we said our goodbyes to Daddy, I saw the three very sad faces of kiddos who would rather have Daddy stay and play than have to wave goodbye to him for a three-day business trip.

Never fear! I had a plan!

After we were all properly sunscreened, hatted, and hydrated, we went into the backyard for a swim. Well, as I mentioned, we had a new puppy. Golden retrievers are water dogs, and Grace thought that whenever anyone got near the pool, she, too, was invited in for a swim. The only problem was that she thought the kids were flotation devices or fetch toys. As I struggled with keeping Grace off the younger two, Ethan, who had been swimming like a fish for a couple of years now, chose that day to figure out that when he went underwater, he could no longer hear my instructions. The first time or two he did this was, in all honesty, quite humorous. After all, he was learning a new way to eventually annoy his mother!

But after repeating my instructions to him four or five times, it rapidly became less and less funny and more and more irritating—especially since I was dealing with two screaming babies and a dog that had mistaken their cries and flailing arms as personal invitations to play with even more bounce and spunk! Eventually, I got everyone out of the pool, and we made our way into the house for lunch and rest time.

But I must not be as bright as I look, because after resting, we ventured back outside again. This time our neighbors joined us. Mike and Terri are wonderful people who love our children and don't have any children of their own. Grace was so happy that not only did we have company, but the company was playing with her and there were kids running everywhere.

Emma and Elliott weren't really on board with the whole swim-without-crying-constantly idea. So I made an executive decision to go inside. My teacup was gaining momentum. As I was telling—check that—as I was *trying* to tell Ethan the new game plan, he insisted on going underwater every time I opened my mouth.

Mike and Terri were crying with laughter. I wasn't nearly as amused.

Kids are such intuitive little machines. They know when Mommy or Daddy is running low on energy or patience, and they don't hesitate to use that to their advantage.

After getting the babies out of the pool and sufficiently dried off, I stationed them by the back door and went back to the water's edge for Ethan, who was still doing a very good impression of a bobbing apple. He was quite pleased with himself until I got back in the pool, picked him up out of the water, and carried him over to the towels.

What came next can only be described as a meltdown of epic proportions that could have easily been followed by "I would like to thank the Academy . . ." Meanwhile, the babies opened the back door and stepped slowly into the house in utter speechlessness and amazement at the massive fit their older brother was throwing.

Emma stared, a bit in awe that it was Ethan putting on the elaborate show. She was usually my drama queen. Elliott stood in silence, waiting to see how this was going to end. Please bear in mind that although we were technically in the house, we weren't far enough in that I could close the back door, which gave Grace yet another invitation to become part of the action.

In she came, bounding into me and a wilting Ethan, sliding across my kitchen tile, wet and muddy tail wagging, and jumping on Emma, who let out her own award-winning shriek. This brought Mike out of the pool to corral Grace back outside while trying (unsuccessfully) to hide a large grin and unconvincing cough cover-up.

Spinning teacups.

Have you ever tried to pick up a wet, screaming four-year-old who didn't want to be picked up? I probably would have had more luck with a thirty-five-pound blob of Jell-O. "Slippery when wet" came to my mind. The "limp noodle" thing that kids do is highly effective. I had to resort to throwing a beach towel over Ethan and scooping him up like I would a wild animal I was trying to get out of the house.

This, let me assure you, wasn't something he expected, nor was it something he welcomed. It was a miracle that both of us made it up the stairs in one piece! By the time I managed to put him in his room and make him stay there, the other two had awoken from their shock and scrambled up the stairs to see what more would take place in this recent battle of wills between Mommy and Ethan.

I was dripping wet, my heart racing. I was very disappointed that the fun day I'd planned was rapidly going from bad to worse. So I did what any levelheaded mother in a very frustrating situation would do: I put in a movie for the other two and told them to stay put. I closed the gate at the top of the stairs and took the baby monitor outside with me so I could apologize to my neighbors for the elaborate show.

As soon as I stepped outside, Grace bounded over, just as happy as ever to see me. Mike and Terri lost all composure, not even trying to hold back the laughter. Seeing them having such a good chuckle lightened my mood slightly and I laughed too.

Terri looked at me. "You know I love your kids, but it is times like this that make me really glad we can go home to an empty house!"

I asked if I could go with her. She laughed even harder.

Thanks to the wonders of modern technology, I heard the ever-present and all-too-familiar cry of "Mommy!" I wanted so badly to answer back with "She's not here!"

My short-lived break was over, and I had to retreat back into the house, back into the duties that I couldn't hand off to anyone else because Daddy was gone for the next three days. My heart sank a little lower in my chest. It turned out that Emma and Elliott had, in fact, snapped out of their momentary loss of speechlessness and peaceful coexistence. My little piranha, who we affectionately refer to as Elliott, had taken a bite out of his sister over a toy of some sort. Emma had more teeth marks on her than Grace's favorite chew toy. You'd think she would have learned not to let him get that close to her!

Once that issue was resolved (a Care Bear Band-Aid on the

finger seemed to cure the bite on her arm), Ethan opened his door and announced that he was ready to be good. And also, he would like to have spaghetti for dinner. Since I had no other plans for dinner, spaghetti worked for me too.

In our house, and I would wager that in most houses where toddlers live, spaghetti is a finger food. But clearly, Emma had been paying a little too much attention to the way Grace ate her food because this was the night she began sucking her spaghetti off her plate. Elliott promptly followed suit. By then, I had neither the energy nor the inclination to stop this madness. They were eating—they weren't fighting—and that was all that mattered to me at that point.

But once dinner was over, the chaos resumed.

Will this ride ever stop?

The kids had gotten into this bad habit of chasing each other through the downstairs while I cleaned the kitchen. It had become a nightly ritual. It wasn't safe and it wasn't something Jeff and I condoned, but on this particular night, I lacked the strength to stop it. As the kids were running (and I do mean running), there was a collision—several to be exact. They ran into each other, they ran into the walls, and they even bumped into the island in the middle of the kitchen floor. I heard cries of annoyance and mild irritation but nothing major.

Naturally, about this time the phone rang. It was Daddy calling to check in. *Where do I even begin?* I was talking to him for all of fifteen seconds when I heard Ethan's voice from the other room—"I'm sorry I'm sorry I'm sorry"—followed by *that* scream.

You know the scream I'm talking about, the blood-curdling scream that comes from the place so deep within your child that he can't move, and it's usually accompanied by breath holding. I hung up on my husband and found Elliott facedown on the tile, Ethan standing beside him, and Emma just rounding the corner to check out the action.

I lashed out at my oldest while picking up the baby from the floor (fully expecting to see blood, but thankfully, there was none). "What did you do to him?"

Not one of my bright and shining moments of motherhood. "Nothin'" was the first answer I got. But as I dragged him once more up the stairs, he told me he might have pushed his little brother down.

Judging from the massive knot forming over Elliott's left eye, I would say "body slam" was a more accurate description. After Ethan was securely placed in his room again, I turned my attention to the purple lump swelling on Elliott's head. He had stopped crying and was now whimpering.

Ice. He needed ice on his head. So I put some frozen peas in a Ziploc sandwich bag and rubber-banded them in a cloth diaper. Remarkably, he kept them on his head for a while. I took both him and Emma upstairs to Emma's room and propped him up on pillows to watch *Aladdin* so I could go explain to Ethan why body-slamming his little brother wasn't a good idea.

After that, I went back downstairs to finish cleaning up the kitchen. I was almost done. I thought I could see the light at the end of the tunnel that was my day when I heard Ethan from the top of the stairs: "Mom, the babies made a mess in Elliott's room with the peas!"

I told him that I would be there in a minute. I wiped the counter. I got cups out of drawer to make their nighttime milk.

"Mom!" This came from Emma. "Elliott poo-poo in my bed!"

I froze.

And thought, *Please God, what are you trying to do to me today?*

Spinning teacups.

I asked Ethan if Elliott still had on a diaper. He said he did, but there was still poo-poo in Emma's bed and I needed to come upstairs right away. I grabbed a plastic grocery bag from the pantry and headed upstairs to see what was waiting for me.

When I walked into Emma's room, I found that the big upset was a chocolate milk stain and Elliott wasn't even dirty. As I turned to leave, I noticed five or six peas on the floor and remembered that Ethan told me there were more in Elliott's room. I figured since I was already upstairs, I might as well go and pick them up; after all, I did have the grocery bag with me.

When I reached the door of Elliott's room, I stopped dead in my tracks. "Mess" didn't even come close to what was waiting for me. It looked as though a bomb of once-frozen peas had exploded all over the place. I didn't think I had put that many peas in the baggie. Apparently I did. I dropped to my knees and began the tedious task of picking up peas one at a time. Enter Emma and Elliott, followed by Ethan saying, "See, I told you there was a mess in here."

Well, Emma and Elliott wanted to "help." But unfortunately, what they did was anything but. As they walked across the room, the peas that were once frozen had now thawed out, making them much easier to squish as they were stepped on by chubby little feet. My patience was gone. I yanked Elliott up and put him in the rocking chair in his room and sent Emma, rather forcefully, to her room. Then I returned to picking up the peas.

The phone rang.

Remember the missing shoe? It was Nana calling to ask me if I had looked for it, and if so, had I managed to find it? Simple question. Justified question. Way wrong time for me to answer it calmly. I snapped at her, informing her that, no, I had not found it and, yes, I had looked for it, along with my neighbors and Ethan.

The only thing I hadn't done was dig up the sandbox, which was the only logical place it could have been, but considering we were talking about a puppy, the word "logical" didn't really seem to fit.

I told her that I had asked Ethan to dig up the sandbox, to which he replied, "But, Momma, what am I supposed to do with the sand after I take it out of the sandbox?"

I assured Nana I would dig it up tomorrow, and we would find the missing shoe.

Pause. Breathe.

I apologized and told her what I was in the process of doing and why, and that I would talk to her later. I hung up and resumed my pea-picking adventure. Fifteen minutes later, I was pretty sure I had found all the peas and had tucked them safely away in the plastic grocery bag.

Then it got fun. I want you to have a good, clear mental picture of this: Holding the top of the bag in one hand, I took hold of the bottom of the bag and gave it a good spin so I could tie the top of it in a knot. Well, unbeknownst to me, the bag had a hole in it just big enough for—you guessed it—peas to fit through. The dozens of peas I had just picked up were back all over the floor.

And my teacup spins faster . . .

Elliott rushed to my rescue, and in the process of "helping" me, he smashed the soft peas into my beige carpet, leaving tiny green spots everywhere. This reduced me to tears. Peas! Again, I got all of them picked up, but this time I was holding the escaped peas in my hand while I headed downstairs to finish the other tasks I had started hours ago and never managed to finish. Finally, after many attempts, the kids were finally in bed. There are no words to describe how tired I was.

As I was getting the house and dogs ready for bed, I opened the back door to let the dogs inside, and something just off the edge of the patio caught my eye: Nana's missing shoe! You would have thought I had discovered the cure for cancer. I was so excited that something had gone right. I raced over and picked it up to examine it—perfect condition. Not a tooth mark on it. Grace had merely hidden it for safekeeping.

When Daddy returned home a few days later, the kids put their angel faces on again. And Nana got her shoe back. The moral of this story is this: No matter how hard you try to make your own plans, kiddos have their own agenda, and that usually doesn't coincide with yours.

Oh, and don't wear your favorite and irreplaceable shoes to a house with three kids, a swimming pool, and a new puppy.

When we were at Disney World, we also rode the bumper cars. The kids had a ball slamming into each other. I was a nervous wreck just watching them.

When you're on a bumper car track, it's impossible to watch everyone else who might be coming your way. Out in public, parents with three or more children face the same challenge. When you and your spouse have two children, you are still operating on a man-to-man defense. Meaning: one kid per one adult. But when you throw a third kid into that mix, you're outnumbered, and you begin operating on a zone defense. Meaning: one parent per two kids.

This is where we found ourselves while at a birthday party when we were potty-training Elliott. Jeff was in the pool with Ethan, because let's face it, Ethan was the easy one. I was supposed to be watching the babies. I was watching them—to an extent. I knew approximately where they were. They both had proper pool floatie suits on, plus there were scores of other parents, so if one of the kids wandered to the poolside, I would know or someone would grab them.

Well, Elliott was more elusive than I gave him credit for. I was caught up in a conversation with another parent when suddenly the hostess mom tugged on my arm to alert me to the exact location of my son.

He was standing in the middle of her patio, shorts around his ankles, peeing on the stick of the umbrella that was stuck through one of her tables. I thought parents were supposed to be able to embarrass their kids, not the other way around. It has been years since that happened, and it still gets brought up at pool parties we attend. They make absolutely sure we know where the bathrooms are. Some people are so funny . . .

As it turns out, Elliott and Ethan weren't the only ones who could blindside me with their antics. Emma turned in a whopper of her own. She just chose a much more elegant setting. Picture this: one black-tie wedding, three precious children (two in miniature tuxedos and one in a dress perfectly crafted to match the bride), and one dignified and tastefully decorated reception hall. What could possibly go wrong?

Have you ever heard the phrase "Looks like country has come to town"? It refers to when the less refined section of society mingles with those more accustomed to shiny, sparkly karats than to dirty orange carrots fresh from the ground.

At any rate, we fell into the category of "Who invited *them?*" This doesn't bother me. I typically don't have too much trouble adjusting to higher society. I prefer real people, but when I must, I can sit at a formal dinner and look presentable. I know which fork to use—the movie *Pretty Woman* was most helpful in that regard—and I know how to make intelligent small talk. My children, though, were too young to realize that there are some things many people in this particular setting would frown (greatly) upon.

My brother-in-law was getting married. He and his bride-to-be sweetly asked Jeff and me if the kids could be in the wedding party. Naturally, we said yes. I was thrilled to be going to such a fancy affair. I love getting dressed up and looking like a girl instead of the tired mommy I parade around as most days.

The kids looked great for their big event too. Emma was the perfect picture of a little princess. The boys did their part very well during the ceremony. No one fidgeted too much. Emma was one of two flower girls, and I'm excited to say that the "accident puddle" that appeared on the floor in the general vicinity of my daughter was not her doing. It was the other flower girl. The wedding went smoothly. No one passed out. I took a deep breath.

Then we moved from the chapel to the reception hall. This place was beautiful. The floor-to-ceiling windows overlooked a magnificent garden backed by some of the tallest trees East Texas has to offer. The whole place could have been a movie set. Inside the room, off to one side, was a huge, curved staircase, where the bride and groom would make their grand entrance down to the reception. This was not a sit-down dinner, but rather many different stations along each wall. Some had fruit, others had veggies, and still others had sweets.

Next to the fruit station was a chocolate fountain, where my children spent most of their time. Heading toward the fountain, I came upon a small crowd of people near the foot of the stairs. Being the nosey woman that I am, I moved closer to investigate. I was met by the wedding coordinator, my new sister-in-law, her mother (who looked like she had eaten something bitter every time she saw me), the wedding photographer, some other random people, and a couple of well-dressed little boys.

The spectacle that everyone was gawking at? A lovely miniature vision in a white flower girl's dress doing her best swan dive from the fifth step of that beautiful curved staircase.

She hit the floor with a resounding smack!

The photographer turned to the crowd in general and announced, "I got it that time!" The wedding coordinator, my brand-new sister-in-law, and her ill-tempered mother all turned to look at me as I stared down at my laughing daughter, lying spread-eagle on the floor.

I opened my mouth, but nothing came out. I swallowed, squared my shoulders, and said, "Someone should go find her father." I spun on my heels, hiked up my dress, stepped over my laughing child, and went in search of the champagne fountain, figuring it would taste better than chocolate.

5.

Alien Adventures and Other UFOs

Have you ever looked at your child and thought, *Where in the world did he come from?* Or, *There's no way she can possibly be mine.* Or, *They don't do anything the way I do. They don't act the way that I do. I never did any of the wretched things they do, I'm absolutely sure.*

Oh, really?

When we get married and decide to have these wonderful little miracles running around our house, we forget that it isn't only our DNA coursing through their little bodies. Granted, you may have been the poster child for the perfect children found in fairy tales. But what about your cousin Irvine on your mother's side, twice removed, who shows up at the family reunion and insists upon wearing the muumuu he bought when he went to Hawaii in 1968 because it feels breezy when the wind blows?

Did you forget about him? His DNA is hardwired into your makeup as well as into Junior's. And that will make for one interesting child concoction. Betcha forgot to mention your dear sweet old cousin Irvine to your hubby before y'all thought about procreation. It is precisely those obscure (and some not so obscure—for example, your mother) relatives I want to bring to your attention.

Alien adventures. Sometimes it most certainly feels like we have entered a parallel universe. I watch, well, I don't actually watch, but I do have the privilege to listen to a lot of *Star Wars* at my house, especially since Disney bought the franchise. I confess: I have never really gotten all that into it. I can't keep track of who belongs on which side, but my oldest son—now he can tell you exactly who fights for the Republic and who fights for the Empire (which, by the way, I had to run downstairs and verify while I was typing this out). There are times when I simply have to stand back and shake my head at the whole lot of them!

The upside to the *Star Wars* thing is the interest in space that has been sparked in my house. Space . . . the final frontier. I know I'm mixing my science fiction metaphors a bit, but bear with me for a minute. I do know that particular line comes from *Star Trek*, not *Star Wars*—but the bottom line is that space is really, really big. Our families can be really, really big as well.

In the beginning, the boys were concerned that remnants of the Death Star would be falling into our swimming pool at any moment until I assured them that it was blown up somewhere over New York State and we were perfectly safe down here in Texas. Then they were fine.

Perhaps I should have been more troubled by their lack of concern for the folks up in New York than I was at the time. I apologize to our friends from the north. But it was through their curiosity of the Death Star that they became very interested in other things that might be in our solar system. Things a bit more real.

It occurred to me that while this was an awesome teachable moment for my boys, it was also a teachable moment for me as a parent. Now, don't panic. I'm not going to turn this into a long, drawn-out analogy of the science class that many of us slept through in high school the first time around. I promise to make this fun. We all just might learn a little something along the way.

Did you know that things are still being discovered in our solar system? Well, when I say "discovered," I am not talking *yesterday*, but I do mean recently, some even in my lifetime, and contrary to what my children think, it wasn't all that long ago. For instance, Pluto wasn't discovered until 1930. That was less than one hundred years ago! When you compare one hundred years to the age of the universe, that's like the blink of an eye.

Jupiter's rings weren't discovered until 1979, which does happen to be in my lifetime. Then in 2006, an astute group of brainiacs got together and decided on the "official" qualifications of a planet, leading to poor Pluto being disqualified as a real planet. He was downgraded to a "dwarf" planet. Can I get a collective "Oooohhhh"? If they were looking for something to occupy their time with, they should have called me. I've got loads of stuff for them . . . literally loads. They could have done my laundry, rather than sit around trying to figure out the exact qualifications of a planet.

Stay with me as we move from the textbook-science realm of discovery to the more abstract. What do my findings have to do with parenting? Plenty. We can start with discovery. How many new talents and abilities have you discovered since you became a parent? I mentioned that I learned how to do many things one-handed. The household chores don't stop because you've got a hungry baby.

Dishes still need to be loaded into the dishwasher. Even as high-tech as that machine is, it won't open the door by itself, jump up, and load those dishes from the sink. My husband calls my way of loading the dishwasher "Dish Tetris." He even gives me points for how many dishes I can shove in there without stacking.

I discovered after having my children that I can hear sounds normal human beings can't, and when I say "normal," I mean male. I can hear a baby crying from the neighbor's house through two closed front doors with televisions on in both houses. The amazing thing about this feat is that my husband (bless his heart) was in the same house as the crying child and couldn't hear said baby wailing. "I thought he was playing," says Hubby. Yep. Playing. He does that. The purple and red blotches on his face are happy colors that emerge as he tries to get your attention.

Just like with Jupiter, I discovered that I had new rings too—although I wasn't nearly as excited about mine as scientists were about Jupiter's. My rings began to appear in 2001—under my eyes. At first I thought my makeup remover was cheap and not doing its job. Then as the days and weeks wore on, I began to slowly comprehend the situation.

It was much, much, much worse than unremoved makeup. My new rings were permanently placed under my eyes. They were dark, they were purple, and they weren't going anywhere. I had to apply concealer before *and* after my foundation to cover the atrocities that sleep deprivation was perpetrating on me. (Almost twenty years later, those rings are still with me, even though the newborns aren't so "new" anymore.)

Speaking of sleep, I'd like to reverse all the mean things I ever said to my mother and preschool teacher every time they tried to get me to take a nap when I was a kid. Unfortunately, you can't stockpile sleep minutes and then make withdrawals as you need them. It would be totally cool if you could, though. I can think of plenty of times I would have made one of those withdrawals.

Like the day when the kids were older and I was struggling after two nights of interrupted sleep. It started when my youngest son decided to read a book just before bed that involved a giant six-foot-tall man-eating rat. That should make for peaceful sleep, don't you think? In the middle of the night, I got a tug on my arm. "Mom, are you awake?" I jolted out of a dead sleep and jumped two feet in the air. Of course I was awake. How could I not be awake at—check the clock—three-thirty in the morning?

"I had a bad dream."

You think? A giant six-foot-tall man-eating rat that happens to guard some distant castle where a princess is being held captive was giving him nightmares? I never would have guessed it. So into bed with my husband and me he came.

Let's just pause right there. My husband and I have never shared a bed with our children. Only under extreme circumstances were they allowed to sleep in our room, and that was on a pallet on the floor. Having a child in our bed meant that the child was between my husband and me. This is not a healthy dynamic for any marriage—more about that later.

But at three-thirty that morning, Elliott climbed over me and into bed between the two of us, and no one got any sleep for the rest of the night. I made an executive Mom decision to ban all books about giant man-eating rats and decreed that nighttime reading had to be benign with bunnies and butterflies to avoid upsetting the delicate sleep patterns that belonged to Mom.

I thought I had done a fairly good job with my new marching orders until the tug the next night. "Mom, are you awake?" I rolled over and peeled the sandpaper off the inside of my eyelids and looked into the face of a different child. Emma. "I had a bad dream." *Man-eating rats?* I wondered.

I looked at the clock: three-fifteen. Awesome. I was beginning to think the kids were holding nightly meetings to see whose turn it would be to poke the sleeping monster. Evidently, Emma had drawn the short straw.

I was also discovering that while they seemed to believe that I didn't require sleep, my husband (who also doubles as their father) had the ability to morph into an invisible and supremely evasive nocturnal being with powers so stealthy he could evade capture by the aliens that had invaded our once peaceful and quiet habitat. In other words, they never woke up Daddy!

Out of bed I came, taking Emma by the hand, and together we walked back up the stairs and into her room. Fool me once, shame on you; fool me twice, shame on me. I was not going to have a kiddo in bed with me two nights in a row. We made it to her room, turned on a night-light, and got the standard, magical drink of water. Then I tucked her back into bed. Just so you don't think I am positively the meanest mother in the world, I did sit with her for a while, stroking her hair until she was almost asleep.

After checking on the boys, I made my way down the stairs to tumble back into bed to rest my eyes for another forty-five minutes before my alarm launched into song, reminding me that is was time to greet the day. My husband merely groaned as he rolled over, still lost in peaceful and undisturbed slumber. How does he do it?

When my kids were babies, Jeff and I decided that it was best for me to stay home with them. I went from working full-time to staying home full-time with three itty-bitty, teeny-tiny little ones that cried constantly. Yes, this was what I had asked for, but where was the fun? Where were the happy babies who played by themselves? Why were my kids always sick? Why was my husband not instantly bonding with our kids? They were his kids too.

I wanted—no, check that—I *craved* adult interaction. I talked to my kids all day long, but there simply wasn't much conversation to be had with a two-year-old. I was feeling like Pluto. I had been downgraded. I was a dwarf planet, stuck in the outermost realm of my solar system—alone, freezing, and wallowing in self-pity. I resembled something that looked like other women, but my qualities were somehow less than. Or so I thought.

This is where the pharmaceutical intervention came into play. My thoughts and feelings of less than were a combination of the hormonal chemical warfare raging inside my body combined with two years of sleep deprivation. I became delusional.

I knew the plan and the path I was on was the right one. It was the path God had ordained for me. It was the path and the plan Jeff and I had discussed and decided would work best for our family. I mean, seriously, look at the cost of day care for three infants. Infants often cost more than children from toddler age and up. My entire paycheck would have gone straight to day care.

(Aside from the cost, most facilities are only legally allowed a maximum of two infants at a time per adult caregiver. Since most day cares have at least one infant already, it's likely that the kids would have ended up in three different places for a few years.)

The majority of my feelings of "downgraded-ness"—is that even a word?—could be solved by a trip to my doctor and a nap. I look back on those early years when all the kids were so little (after I break into a cold sweat) and think about the memories I missed. I was so tired. I never slept. The whole house seemed to be in survival mode.

Along with the alien adventures of parenting comes something else: *close encounters of the third kind*, better known as extended family and in-laws.

When I thought I was in labor with my daughter (there were a couple of false alarms in there), Jeff and I spent one night walking the floors of the hospital. I really wanted Emma out. I was ready to *not* be pregnant anymore. Emma really likes to be in control. Wonder where she gets that from? She liked it that way while I was pregnant, and she still likes it that way today. The apple certainly doesn't fall far from the tree.

Anyway, as I was walking the halls, I wanted to talk to my mother, a perfectly natural request. I didn't have my cell phone with me, but that was all right because Jeff had his. I was flipping through his contact list looking for my mother's name and growing more frustrated. This is the problem with speed dial.

When I was a kid, I knew everyone's name and number by heart. Now I have them in my phone, and if I call you all the time, you are in my "favorites," so I really don't even have to remember your last name. At the time of my floor-pacing episode with Emma, I couldn't find my mother's name. Don't panic—I do remember her last name—even her first name on certain days.

I didn't expect my husband to have her listed in his phone under "Mother," but after several minutes of searching everywhere else, accompanied by several fairly strong contractions and a fuse that was burning faster by the second, I threw the phone at him and shouted, "I want to talk to my mother! I know you have her in there! Where is she?"

He righted the phone (he'd barely been able to catch it before it hit the ground) and calmly scrolled through his contact list. In a matter of seconds, he handed it to me and said, "Baby, she's right here. Under 'Outlaw.'"

I just stared at him. Looking back, I can see the humor and the appropriateness of the nickname. It totally fits, but at the time, on that night, it wasn't funny.

To survive parenting, it's wonderful to have access to as many generations as possible. When my kids were born, they were the fifth living generation on my side of the family. It was super cool. There is no a handbook on what to do with that many people. What do you do when you all get together? How do you talk to everyone? What happens if members of one generation begin to lose their mind?

Even though my kids were the fifth generation, within a matter of a couple of years, our family quickly slimmed down to only two generations. We lost some matriarchs soon after my youngest was born—first my great-grandmother and then my grandmother—and my grandfather died shortly after that. Those last two were the parents of my mother—the Outlaw. Well, having both of her parents gone on ahead to glory, my mother decided to make some changes. Changes that I never in a million years saw coming.

I come from a long line of self-employed folks. We are driven. We are hard workers. My parents are no exception. For the past twenty-five years, my parents have been a staple in north Austin (that's in Texas, y'all) with not one, but two highly successful restaurants. One of them was the Little Deli, which started as a moveable trailer in a parking lot. It was the bane of my exis-tence in middle school. I was sentenced to work there every day throughout the summers, and then my sentence was extended to after school once I passed my driver's test.

From the humble beginnings of that little trailer, they moved into a more permanent space in the shopping center where they had previously held only a spot in the parking lot. Business boomed. Several years later, a new restaurant space opened up down the road from their house, and they converted that into a quaint, little Italian neighborhood eatery. Thankfully by the time It's Italian opened, I had already moved to Houston and could no longer be forced into schlepping drinks or carrying heavy food-laden trays.

My three younger sisters, though, weren't so lucky. My parents hired all three of them for various roles in both locations and prided themselves on being family owned and operated. Both restaurants were critically acclaimed all across Austin. The *Austin-American*

Statesman newspaper wrote articles about the food, the charm, and the ambiance of both places. Life was busy, but it was good. Then one afternoon, I received a phone call from my mother.

Me: Hello?

Mother (in very excited voice): I have wonderful news!

Me: Okay. (I muffled the phone.) Ethan don't throw that—

Mother: We sold the Deli!

Me: (Choke.) You did what?

Mother: We sold the Deli! Tony from down the street bought it!

Me: Mother, are you ill? Where's Dad? Does he know about this?

Mother: Yes! We sold the restaurant too!

Me: (I walked into my room, closed the door, and sat on the floor.) Why?

Mother: We put the house on Craigslist.

Me: Mother, don't move. I'm coming.

Mother: Why? I'm fine. Your dad and I are going to truck-driving school.

Me: I'm sorry—you're going to do *what*?

Mother: Truck-driving school. We're going to become big rig truckers.

Me: Again, Mom, I have to ask. *Why?*

Mother: Well, we want to see the country. An RV is too expensive. This way we get paid. Oh, and we're sending your youngest sister to Houston to live with you.

I hung up.

Close encounters of the third kind.

Who does something like that? Who walks away from a successful business of twenty-five years to become an over-the-road trucker? My parents. They did go to truck-driving school. I didn't know there were schools for that. Kind of made me feel better, though. I see those big rigs on the road, all eighteen wheels turning. It's nice to know the drivers have been shown how to drive.

I asked my mother if the trucking company would block the gas pedal for her—my mom stands in at barely five feet tall. She didn't think that was very funny. I did. They bought a huge fire-engine-red semitruck.

The house didn't sell on Craigslist—thankfully. They had to enlist the help of an actual realtor. But that left a couple of loose ends, three to be exact. I have three younger sisters. My sisters are much, much younger than I am. Mother was totally not kidding when she said she was sending the youngest to Houston. Jeff and I could have said no right there on the spot, but I honestly thought somewhere in my mind that having Kristina around would be, could be, fun.

So my twenty-year-old baby sister really did move in. There is most certainly a reason God gives our children to us as babies and not as twenty-year-olds. If they came to us as twenty-year-olds, our population would be on a significant and irrevocably rapid decline. I love my sister. Amazingly enough, I still love my sister, but there were times during her incarceration—I mean her stay here with us—that I envisioned mailing pieces of her back to my parents.

Kristina was supposed to be with us for about nine or ten months. That would have been long enough to attend cosmetology school and get a license in hair design. Eighteen months later, due to a slight lack of focus, she hadn't finished school and thus no license had been acquired. I didn't have the help around the house I had been promised before her arrival, and on top of all this, I had yet another body to clean up after and one more mouth to feed.

My Mom Radar would go off between two and three o'clock every morning, alerting me to the fact that she still hadn't made it home, which kicked into high gear the worry factor and the hallucination stage of the "what would my mother do to me if something happened to my sister on my watch?" phase. Close encounters of the third kind—the party-all-night kind.

By this point, my parents and my other two sisters had decided to set up their home base in sunny San Diego (which could get its own chapter for close encounters—I like California, but Texans and Californians are very different). With the most diplomatic tone I could muster, I called my mother and told her that if she wanted her youngest daughter in one reusable piece and not a bag of confetti, she needed to point that big rig in the direction of Houston and come get her.

My nerves simply couldn't handle being the parent of a now twenty-one-year-old. I had my hands full with my six-, seven-, and eight-year-old kids, even though the behavior among the four of them was really quite similar. Bottom line: My sister joined the rest of my family, and since then, I have been all by myself in Texas. My entire immediate family is fourteen hundred miles away in California. Roll theme music: "All by Myself" . . . fade out. I crack myself up.

If you thought it was just the family on my side who was going to be compared to extraterrestrial life forms, guess again. Oh no. My sweet mother-in-law has also provided me with ample material. Carol lived with us for about a year and a half, and the help that she afforded me during that time provides her with a fair amount of immunity when it comes to ribbing. With that said, one area of her life is simply too good to pass up.

Around the same time my parents took a leap off the midlife-crisis cliff, it became abundantly clear that they called Carol and had her drink the same Kool-Aid. I swear it was within a couple of months of receiving my mother's phone call that Jeff came home looking as though he had been hit by a bus. With a lump in my throat and a knot in my stomach, I asked him what had happened, thinking maybe someone had died.

He said, "Mom bought a bike."

In all of my wisdom and naiveté, I thought, *Hmm, that's nice. She can get some exercise. It'll be good for her.* And that's what I told Jeff.

He stared back at me with a blank expression. "No, babe. A bike. A motorcycle. Like a Harley. But she didn't get a Harley and doesn't like them, so don't ever, ever confuse her Honda with a Harley."

Again, I had to sit down. Close encounters of the third kind. What was going on with my family?

Carol took a motorcycle safety class the very first weekend she had her bike. For that, I was grateful. At least both sets of grandparents were into the safety thing! The kids thought the fact the Nana rode a motorcycle and Granny and Papaw drove a big rig was just too cool for words. Jeff and I wondered when, exactly, our roles had been reversed—when did we become the responsible ones, the parents of our parents?

Come to find out, you don't simply own a motorcycle. To really understand the bike, you have to become one with the bike, and to do that, you must be able to take it completely apart and then (ideally) put it back together with few leftover parts. Soon, I began saving my gallon milk jugs, not for the igloo projects my children built once a year at school, but for the breakdown parties Nana held at her house. They needed something to drain the oil into, and milk jugs seemed to work the best. Who knew?

Carol got connected with a "chapter" (my guess is that it's a group of other folks who ride), and they go tooling around the Texas Hill Country. I'm glad she doesn't go out alone much. I'm a huge believer in the old saying "There's safety in numbers."

She knows how to handle her bike. She wears her protective

gear, and we keep buying her new helmets for Christmas, not because she wears them out (thankfully) but because she wants the latest and greatest, and she pays attention. That's about as good as we can expect.

I can honestly tell you that, without a doubt, I didn't see this type of alien adventure coming my way: truck drivers and motorcycle people. Does it get any crazier than that?

UFOs in space are widely talked about. I don't believe that little green men are flying around in spaceships, but I also didn't think my parents or my mother-in-law would do what they did either. So, really, what do I know?

The UFOs I want to talk are different. I call them "unique family occasions." Anytime you mix two different bodies of people together, interesting things are going to happen. Can I tell you that I'm tickled pink Jeff doesn't spook easily? The very first time I brought him home to meet my family was a nightmare by female standards. He took it in stride—I was mortified.

I met Jeff while I was living in Houston. My entire family, as you now know, lived in Austin. Within a couple of dates, I knew I had met my perfect match—he was "the one," my Prince Charming—pick a cliché. I was going to have to take him home to meet the parents sooner or later. We had been dating for about three weeks when I called my mother and told her I was coming home for the weekend and bringing Jeff with me. She was shocked speechless.

I hadn't brought anyone home in years. Literally. She wanted to know if I had drugged him. (To know my mother is to love her.) I begged her not to scare him off and to please have Daddy be on his best behavior. As we were on the road making the two-and-a-half-hour trip from Houston to Austin, my cell phone rang.

My mother. She wanted me to know how excited she was to see us and that there might be "a few people" at the house when we arrived.

My heart sank. I know my parents. At this point in their lives, they were heavily engrossed in the restaurant and catering business. Anytime Mother mentioned "a few," that could easily be translated into at least fifty. I wanted to turn around, but we were more than halfway to Austin, so we kept going.

When we got to my parents' subdivision, I was desperately trying to remain calm. I had a couple of different factors working against me, the first being that they hadn't lived in this house for very long and my sense of direction is dismal at best. I didn't want to tell my new boyfriend that I was unsure about where my parents actually lived.

The second factor went hand in hand with the first. When we turned into their section of the subdivision, I thought we were on the wrong street because both sides were lined with cars. There wasn't an empty driveway or a vacant spot in front of any house to be found.

Without being able to see the houses properly, I couldn't tell which house belonged to my parents. Slowly, the weight and the realization of what I was seeing washed over me. All those cars were there because of us! Taking a deep breath, I managed to point and say, "There's a place way over there."

"It looks like someone is having a party," Jeff said.

Yeah. It sure does, I thought. *Should I tell him now? Or should I wait and see what he's really made of? If I tell him now, I may need a ride back to Houston.*

We started walking in the general vicinity of what I hoped to be my parents' house.

"I think all these people might be at Mom and Dad's." I tried to sound casual.

He stopped walking. "Why?"

"Well, I haven't exactly brought anyone home in a long time. I'm sure people are curious. It'll be fine. Just roll with it." I hoped he couldn't feel my hand shaking in his as we continued to get closer to the house.

My parents, thanks to one of my little sisters playing lookout from an upstairs window, met us at the door. My dad shook Jeff's hand and then proceeded to tell him everything he'd learned about him through the background check he had obtained via the internet that morning. He followed it with "Hey, I needed to make sure you weren't a scumbag. She's my daughter, you know."

I looked at my mother for help. She shook her head and pulled us inside. I couldn't believe the people. They were everywhere!

Turns out, no one believed I was bringing anyone home because, as I said, it hadn't happened in so long. Jeff did amazingly well considering he'd had a background check done on him and several Austin Police officers (they frequented the Deli and the restaurant) were there in uniform and wanted to ask him about his driving and criminal record, not to mention he met my grandparents, aunts, uncles, and most of the rest of my extended family.

The absolute icing on the cake was the crowd of people who wanted to know what, exactly, his intentions were and if he did, in fact, plan on marrying me. Was he aware that the ring he put on my finger needed to have a rock big enough to equal one karat for every child he expected me to carry for him? Ouch. That was when I put a straw in a champagne bottle and sat on the couch, waiting for the roast—I mean the party—to be over.

Jeff handled everything in stride. He was flattered by the outpouring of people just for us and marveled at the close-knit family relationships we shared. He didn't seem bothered at all by the great expectation imposed on him by indulgent partygoers. That has to be the primary difference between men and women.

Unique family occasions. Is it any wonder we eloped?

The "uniqueness" didn't stop there. No. It followed us into our married life—right on down the road.

You see, after my experience with the backpack-leash scenario in Orlando, I decided that air travel might not be the best idea for a family of five. We bought a monster SUV, fully loaded with separated seats (so no one could touch each other) and the best invention ever for long car trips—a DVD player! We drove to Florida two or three times in that thing. I lost count. I don't think my brain cells, unlike the cellulite cells in my thighs, are reproducing. We drove to California and back once. I made that trip alone with three kids—proof positive that my brain cells are dying off. And we drove all over Texas, which should count as cross-country travel considering the sheer size of this state.

A few years ago, we went to a mini family reunion on my husband's side. My father-in-law wanted to get together with his three brothers, some of their kids, and us. We thought it would be a hoot, so we farmed out the dogs, loaded into the SUV, and headed up to Kentucky.

I'm blessed to have (for the most part) wonderful in-laws. We all get along relatively well. They are fun and they are funny. Those are two extremely important qualities when you are spending large quantities of time with folks.

For as many times as we crossed state lines with our children, it never ceased to amaze me that one of them would ask something really off the wall (at really inopportune times) in a very loud voice. For example, Emma asked at a Chick-fil-A in Louisiana, "Do they speak English here?" I'm almost certain the people behind the counter didn't think it was funny. (I sort of threw that one in there—even with my horrible sense of direction, I realize that you don't have to drive through Louisiana to get to Kentucky.)

We kept telling the kids it was the Bluegrass State, which intrigued Emma immensely. She was forever on the hunt for *blue* grass. So, because I'm running for Mother of the Year, as we were driving, I would point out the window and say, "Look, Emma! Did you see it? Over there. Blue grass." And she would reply that she hadn't seen it, and then she'd be disappointed until the next time, and we would do it all over again. I can be so mean. The boys didn't seem to care about blue grass in the slightest.

We stayed at this sweet little cabin on a lake near Jeff's uncle's house. It was perfect for us. It had three bedrooms. The boys' room had two twin beds, Emma's room had a full-size bed, and our room had a queen-size bed plus a TV. The thing that blew me away the most was the price: We paid more for a hotel room in Texarkana, Texas, for one night than we did for two nights in our cozy cabin by the lake in Kentucky, and it wasn't a great hotel room in Texarkana! I'm talking one star, maybe two.

Most of the time we were there, my father-in-law, Papa Dan, and his three brothers picked on each other mercilessly. As full-grown adult men, they should have known how to behave. Wrong. It was nothing more than a case of sibling rivalry gone amuck. They told stories of the things they did to each other when they were kids, what they did as younger adults, and even now as grandpas! It was a waste of time and energy to put on my makeup. They had me laughing so hard, I was crying.

Then I got worried. This was in my children's DNA makeup. What in the world were my boys going to do to each other? Heaven help us.

When the conversations got to be too much for the children to handle, we took walks around the property and across the way. When you're out in the country, it's very easy to just go "across the way."

During one of those walks, we decided to do some target practice with a couple of the cousins (because you have those too in the country: "cousins"). We set up a two-by-four across a couple of sawhorses, stood six cans along the board, and walked back about forty yards. Jeff asked the kids who wanted to go first. Ethan's hand shot straight in the air. Jeff then went over some basic rules:

1. Never point a gun at anyone.
2. Always point the barrel to the ground until you're ready to shoot.
3. Always have the safety on until you're ready to shoot.
4. Never handle a gun unless an adult is with you.

Ethan answered each command with a resounding "Yes, sir!" Jeff loaded a little .17 caliber rifle and handed it to Ethan, who was eight at the time. Ethan took his stance, closed one eye, and fired.

BAM! One can down. BAM! Second can down. BAM! BAM! BAM! BAM!

He flipped the safety switch, lowered the barrel to the ground, and slowly handed the gun to his daddy. He didn't even flinch. He hit every single can. I couldn't believe it! This is also the same kid who has an extraordinary fascination with all military tactics and both World Wars. I see the armed forces in his future.

I suppose his sharpshooting skills shouldn't have come as that big of a surprise. We come from a long line of hunters. And in Texas, we do things like hunt for food, hunt for fun, and go to the gun range because there's nothing better to do on a Saturday afternoon. And, yes, I can say "redneck." I *am* one. Evidently my husband and I were raising some little rednecks as well.

As for the other two kids that day: Elliott hit only one can. I'm not a hundred percent sure that the wind didn't knock it over. And Emma wanted nothing to do with that particular pastime. We discovered that she was better with a bow and arrow. She had great form, nice pullback, and great follow-through. Amazingly enough, for her size, she not only hit the target but made the arrows stick.

It's nice to know that when civilization ends, we won't starve. Each one of us brings a little something new and exciting to the table—literally. There's just one problem: I'm the only one who knows how to cook it.

Alien adventures. Close encounters of the third kind. Unique family occasions.

We had another family member you haven't met yet. His name was Nelson, and he was very special to us. Rarely did we go on a road trip without him. A few times we had to leave him behind for logistical reasons. For instance, we didn't take him to Kentucky, but when we stayed in Texas, he was our favorite companion.

Nelson was our travel trailer.

When I married into this family, I knew they were fairly "outdoorsy." Jeff's stepdad loved to camp. Me, not so much. Little did I know that the type of camping Papa Jim did would be redneck luxury at its finest! He was the one who introduced us to our Nelson.

Perhaps you've heard the saying that everything is bigger in Texas. Well, truer words have never been spoken, especially when it came to Nelson. He was a little more than forty feet long and had two bedrooms and two bathrooms, a kitchen and dining area, and a living room big enough for a full-size sleeper sofa. We could have lived in Nelson if we needed to.

Anything that big needed a name. We listen to a lot of country music where I come from, and one of my all-time favorite musicians—really one of the all-time greats of country music—is Willie Nelson. His song "On the Road Again" is the anthem for gypsies everywhere. I didn't want to name this beast Willie, but Nelson had a nice ring to it. Voilà!

Our fondest memories are of hunting season, not because we all rode around on four-wheelers with shotguns just looking for defenseless animals to shoot at, but because we got to enjoy the fellowship that took place between members of my family and the friends who went with us. We were outside all the time. No internet connections. No cable TV. No satellite. No Wii gaming console. Being out and about as a family cemented us together.

The kids played with rocks and sticks and made forts out of cedar tree branches. Then their allergies would bother them for a week, but the point is that they had a blast. They hiked up the hills and searched for nests where the deer might be bedded down during the day. They checked for tracks. They learned how to scope out mesquite trees, looking for "rubs," or places where bucks were rubbing the velvet off their antlers. And the kids learned how to build fires, real fires. They also discovered that those fires burn hot, and they must not touch them. Side note: Each one of them tried one time.

Living in the city has muted our basic survival skills. We have gotten away from the thrill and the joy of being able to do things ourselves and with our own two hands, because we have come to be incredibly dependent on the conveniences of modern technology. Don't get me wrong. I love modern technology! And I enjoy a pedicure just like any other woman. I get my nails done every two weeks. I have to have some girlie vices.

But I believe it's imperative that we teach our children how to be outside. We have to teach them that there is more to life than the latest video game or the latest new pair of shoes.

A whole other world is waiting to be discovered. A world that includes Grannies who drive huge red big-rig trucks and Nanas who ride great big motorcycles. And a world full of dirt and fast-moving creeks. Kids need to be shown the difference between pets and wildlife, between snakes that simply slither and snakes that will land you in the ER.

Parenting is the final frontier. We will be faced with aliens from other worlds disguised as sweet innocents (aka our children). We will have close encounters of a third kind (aka our in-laws). But through it all, if we stick together, we will survive.

6.

It's Fun to Feed a Fish

I haven't made it a secret that I come from the South. Actually, I come from the West *and* the South, which lands me right smack-dab into a whole new category of stereotypes. Down here in Texas, one of our most favorite things in the entire world is duct tape. For the longest time, I thought the word was "duck" tape, as in *quack-quack*, until someone explained to me that it was actually duct, as in an air-conditioning duct. Oh, the things we learn.

At any rate, down here, we use this stuff for everything. It is hands-down one of the most wonderful inventions to hit the hardware shelves since the hammer. We use it for school projects. We can fix broken windows with it. We can even duct-tape a car bumper to hold it in place, as made evident by one of my neighbors . . .

Lately I have noticed that not only does it come in your classic silver, but manufacturers wised up and now make it available in fashion-friendly designs for the female population. You can pick up the ever-popular roll of duct tape in hot pink, bright red, basic black, and even camo green or camo pink. Google "duct tape prom dresses," and I promise your mouth will drop wide open, and then you will need your own roll of duct tape to get it closed again.

Why am I telling you all of this? We have already walked

through using leashes (some call them backpacks) on our kids. I have a very sarcastic sense of humor, and I might have said in the past that all you really need to raise good and obedient kids are leashes and duct tape—but I was kidding.

Duct tape has some excellent and creative uses, but child restraint isn't one of them. On February 17, 2011, a San Bernardino County, California, woman (Danyella Higgins) was arrested for endangering a child (her two-year-old) when she duct-taped the child's hands, feet, and mouth, *took a picture* of the child, and then sent the picture via text message to a friend. The friend quickly called authorities, who were then dispatched to the woman's house.

They found the child unharmed (except for trace pieces of duct tape still clinging to various body parts) and the nineteen-year-old mother spluttering excuses about taping up a window, thinking it would be funny to use duct tape on the baby. The child was removed immediately from her and placed in Child Protective Services custody.

Do you see anything wrong with this picture? I see several things. During this chapter, we will take a look at them all and follow a few rabbit trails along the way. The obvious and screaming question is this: Who duct-tapes their kid? Didn't she know it was wrong? The best answer that I can come up with is no, perhaps she didn't. The mother in question was nineteen years old. She wasn't much more than a baby herself. Chances are no one had ever told her that duct-taping your baby was, in fact, wrong. It sounds very trivial to you and me, but sometimes that's precisely what it boils down to.

Think about this for a minute: How did you learn to tie your shoes? Someone had to show you. Someone had to sit you down and teach you how to loop, swoop, and pull or use the bunny ears to tie your bow. Parenting is the same way. For anyone reading this book right now who has never been told, please *do not* duct-tape your kids. I will help you discipline your kids with more humanity while keeping your sanity intact.

Let me start with a little disclaimer: I have an "old school" background. But please don't let that scare you.

Close to our house is one of those behemoth pet stores. You know the kind. It's bigger than two football fields and smells twice as bad as three locker rooms combined hovering over a moldy swamp. You walk through the automatic sliding doors and your ears are instantly assaulted with the screeches and cries of the caged birds and the spinning wheels of the rat cousins (better known as hamsters).

My children and I entered this utopia one afternoon to buy dog food. I typically didn't bring my young children to the pet store. The temptations were too strong. It's the pet industry's version of the Jedi Force drawing the kids closer and closer to the kennels where the ferrets are kept or the aquariums where the reptiles slither. They just couldn't help themselves.

On that particular day, the Force was apparently working on me too, because when they wanted to go look at the fish, I consented. We left the pet store with our thirty-five-pound sack of dog food and a four-ounce shaker of fish food. The kids had convinced me that our life simply would not be complete without this: the prettiest of little blue fish. Of course, a fish needs a bowl, some fake marine plant life, and a castle to swim in and out of and, finally, some rocks to go on the bottom of the bowl.

Home we went with Flippy secure in Ethan's hands and the other two kids each holding on to something equally treasured so they would feel included in the arrival of Flippy to our house. He was our first fish as a family. Have you ever had a fish? I knew the basics of fish care, but beyond that, we would have to learn as we went.

For starters, I knew that for Flippy's well-being, he (I don't know whether it was a boy or girl) absolutely had to stay in his bowl. That fact was undeniable. Even though we felt sorry for Flippy being stuck swimming around and around and around, looking at the same view over and over and over again, his bowl provided the necessary habitat that was life-sustaining for him. He would die outside his bowl. We moved it from time to time to give him new things to look at, but taking Flippy out of his bowl was out of the question.

Something else I knew about fish was their food. It looks like powder. When you shake it from the box, it floats gently and gracefully down to the surface of the water and hovers there for just a brief moment until the fish come stealthily from underneath to snatch it.

It didn't matter how much food we fed Flippy or how often, he would always eat. This is a highly amusing pastime for children—but lethal for poor Flippy. We set up a schedule of turns for which child could feed Flippy, trying to avoid the unavoidable. This worked for a while.

Over time, though, the Force was too strong and the children's resistance was no match. Flippy's food proved to be too great a temptation, and he became the permanent guest of honor at a Las-Vegas-style, all-you-can-eat buffet. It was a sad, sad day. Flippy quite literally ate himself to death. Why? How? Well, it's fun to feed a fish. But it isn't always the best thing for them. They need boundaries. They need rules—and so do children.

Children need the same safety and security afforded to a fish in a bowl of water. Now, I'm not suggesting you stick your child in a bowl full of water, but hear me out on this. Children need boundaries. Boundaries keep them safe. Without boundaries, kids wander off, stray too far, get into unfamiliar territory, and find themselves unable to breathe.

That said, when our kids were babies, we babyproofed the house. We installed magnetic Tot-Locks on all the kitchen cabinets. Looking back, we could have just put them on the cabinet that held the cleaners. We also made sure every outlet in the house had a plastic cover. Those worked great until the kids figured out how to take them off. Amazingly enough, no one was electrocuted. The best investment in child safety we ever made were the gates at the top and bottom of the stairs.

Aside from those adjustments to the house, everything else stayed the same. The house still belonged to my husband and me. The kids were an added bonus. We didn't want to be one of those couples who had lost the ability to relate to other people simply because we now had a baby (or two or three).

Granted, our living room floor did closely resemble the showroom of FAO Schwartz for a while, but that was to be expected. (Three babies in two years will definitely rearrange your living room.) But the basic structure of the house didn't change. Of course, giving your child these "boundaries" will most assuredly not win you any popularity contests at first, but they will pay off in the end.

Because my kids were babies at the same time, I expected their first word to be "no." It was all I said. Each time one of them would crawl to the stairs, I'd say, "No-no." The dog food bowl was their favorite hangout. But that was always met with "No-no" from me. Dog food is nutritious for dogs, not for babies, even though my kids did eat plenty of it until they figured out it didn't taste very good.

The dog water bowl was another favorite haunt. Many a Weeble wobbled and drowned in it. My pictures on low-lying shelves were under continual attack from the kids. Still, the pictures stayed where they were. I didn't move them.

The one item in the house that drew those kids to it just like ants at a picnic was the cuckoo clock my parents brought back to me from Germany. Cuckoo clocks have long chains that hang down, so the clock itself needs to be hung at least six feet off the ground to give the chains room to move. It's the movement of these chains that actually wind the clock and keep the sweet little cuckoo bird, well, cuckooing.

What could I do with the clock to keep it out of harm's way? Some of my options:

One: Take the clock off the wall instead of having to deal with the continual threat of three kids tugging on the chains.

Two: Move the clock to a more secure location. That way it wouldn't be put away per se, but it would be safer.

Three: Teach the little tricycle motors that this was my house with my things in it, and they had plenty of their own stuff to touch, eat, and destroy. They didn't need to lay their chubby fingers (even though they were incredibly cute chubby fingers) on my cuckoo clock.

I went with option three, and let me tell you why: If our house were the only house my children ever went to, I would be happy to move everything out of their reach. But that isn't realistic. I have friends. I have friends who don't have children. I wanted to be able to take my children with me when I visited their house. Better yet, after visiting their house once with my kids, I wanted to be invited back. We didn't want to move everything in our house four feet up off the ground so Junior couldn't reach it until he was three—because by that time, he would think he owned the house.

That's the same reason I always decorated every part of my Christmas tree. I would tell my kids, "Yes, the tree is beautiful. Yes, it's lovely. Oh, I know you want to touch it, but you mustn't because it isn't yours." Kids are smart. Tell Junior that climbing to the top of the Christmas tree is unsafe and the tree isn't his.

When it comes to priceless family heirlooms, use some common sense. Ornaments that have been passed down from your great-great-great-grandmother may need to either wait for a later date or be placed on the top of the tree. I have my grandmother's nativity scene, which is priceless to me. My kids are well past the "I want to touch everything" stage, but I still put that set where no one can reach it. I would be heartbroken if something happened to it. My grandmother is gone.

Sometimes there's a legitimate reason we tell our children no. Sometimes it's for their own safety. Sometimes the answer is no simply because we said so. Regardless, you are the parent. Stand your ground.

Children are among the smartest criminals—I mean *people*—on the planet. And it starts from a very young age. No one has to teach them how to manipulate a situation. It seems to be already installed into their hardwiring. It's amazing to watch, but mortifying to live through. Allow me to share a page from my "Most Embarrassing Moments" scrapbook.

When Ethan was about ten months old, a different set of in-laws came to visit. Jeff's dad and stepmother, Dan and Linda, flew in from Colorado. They are some of the sweetest people in the world, very laid back, and incredibly nonconfrontational. On their first night in Texas, we decided to go out to dinner. Of course, whenever you take an infant or young child out to eat in public, you run the risk of a nuclear-core meltdown—from the child, one or both parents, or the restaurant staff—or all of the above. On top of that, I was already pretty pregnant with Emma, so between dealing with raging hormones and throwing up everything, I had a short fuse. Can you see where the drama might have room to grow?

At ten months old, Ethan was filled to overflowing with the wiggles. He couldn't sit still for longer than a few minutes. This isn't unusual for most babies, but dealing with it is one of the hardest parts of parenting—bar none. You see, Ethan wanted out of his high chair. I wasn't going to hold him, Jeff wasn't going to hold him, and even though his grandparents would have held him, that wasn't a viable option. We, as the parents, wanted to take this opportunity to teach Ethan that we were in control of the situation, and he wasn't.

He tried to climb out of the high chair, so we used the seat belt to strap him in. Then he began to cry. His grandmother tried to appease him with bread. The kid could have medaled for gold in the shot-put event in the Olympics with the distance he put on those rolls as he chucked them across the restaurant.

I dug into the magic and normally bottomless diaper bag for more tricks. He wasn't interested. Toy after toy after cup after the ultimate weapon—the bottle—which landed on the floor. I picked it up and handed it back to him. He threw it again, and it landed behind us. I picked it up one more—and final—time. For the grand finale, he threw the bottle on the table beside us.

Ethan's cries began to escalate into screams. For those of you who haven't yet experienced this ratcheting up of the volume, just wait. As I mentioned, there is a substantial difference between a crying baby and a screaming one.

Ethan now had his back in a full arch, arms flailing, face beet red, fighting with everything in him against the restraints keeping him in the wooden chair, while his father politely cut the rest of the chicken on his own plate as though nothing was going nuclear beside him. My in-laws were averting their eyes from the scene. I suggested that maybe we should leave.

Enter the manager of the restaurant. "Is there anything I can do to help?"

Jeff looked up at him, smiled, and said, "I could use some more tea. Thanks for stopping by."

Have you ever had that dream where you're walking down the street naked? And everyone can see you? That's where I was at that moment. Jeff was proving a point. A battle of wills was taking place between him and his son. It boiled down to who had the bigger stubborn streak. Turns out, my husband did.

That high chair represented everything Ethan hated about life on that day. He wanted to be free to roam, to play, to dump all the salt on the table, and pull all the little packets of sugar out of their basket. He wanted to sit in the middle of the table and kick his legs and laugh and coo at everyone in the place.

Was there anything so wrong with that? Well, yes, as a matter of fact. For starters, children don't belong on the table. They belong in chairs. Secondly, I mentioned that boundaries need to be set for children's own good and safety—well, what I haven't told you is where we were having dinner. A steak house called Texas Land & Cattle Company. This place had the biggest steak knives I have ever seen. Had we let Ethan out of his chair, even if someone was holding him, he would have been within range of one of those knives. It was for his safety and well-being that he remain in his chair.

Then there's the old standby that just so happens to be my favorite: He needed to be in his chair because that is where we put him, and because we said so.

That was one of the most brutal trips to a restaurant I have ever had to endure. But you know something? It happened just once. The next time we went out to eat, Ethan stayed in his chair.

Not only do kids need boundaries, they want them. It astounds me that our society today is so utterly confused about the role of the parent. I love my children so much it actually hurts sometimes. I'm filled to the point of overwhelming emotion when I watch them sleep or listen to them being sweet to each other or watch them participate in school programs. But I won't let them control me.

I remember one afternoon playing Fish Out of Water with them on the playground of the elementary school around the corner from our house. We had a blast! My husband was tagged twice. Even through all those emotions and fun times, our primary role in their life is one of authority over them. It isn't our job to be their *friend*. It's our job to be their *parent*. There's a big difference between the two.

Let me remind you: Parenting isn't for sissies. It requires strength you never knew you had. You will undergo on-the-job mind-training worthy of Jedi fighters. You will learn how to function on less sleep than prisoners of war in a concentration camp. You will discover that consistency is your secret weapon—it is the key to winning not only the battle but also the entire war.

The goal is to rear good and decent functioning adults. We want to raise our kids to grow into adulthood so they can leave our homes and go into the world to become productive citizens. They need basic skill sets to do this. They need a solid foundation of right and wrong and consequences of their wrong choices or actions. They need an understanding and a healthy respect for those in authority over them.

• • •

We live in a two-story house that's about twenty years old. When it was built, open floor plans were all the rage. We have a large playroom directly over the downstairs living room. You can hear everything that goes on upstairs. I can hear my boys drop a Lego. The staircase, located to one side of the living room, has a wall filled with framed pictures of the family. My pictures go from the railing to as far up as I can reach.

I have three very strong-willed children. I love that about them. I love their spirits and their spunk. Most of the time. But it makes parenting them a challenge. I have to be able to discipline them effectively without breaking their spirits. I want them to know that I mean business, but I can't do that by bullying them, scaring them, or beating them into submission.

Neat trick, right?

As you recall, my daughter is dramatic. Everything is a monumental deal. When she was younger, every time she got mad or got her feelings hurt, she would stomp up the stairs. Emma is a petite little thing, so this shouldn't have been a problem. But then again, dynamite is little too, and we all know what dynamite can do.

As she stomped deliberately on each step, every picture on my wall rattled so terribly I thought they would all come crashing down. This wasn't a new tactic for Emma. And the consequence that followed wasn't new either, even though she acted as though it were.

I waited until she got to the top of the stairs and then called her back down. STOMP—STOMP—STOMP. She wouldn't say anything. She just looked at me. This, too, is unacceptable behavior. So we waited in an Old West–style stand-off.

She was often the first to cave. "Ma'am?" (Yes, we say "ma'am" and "sir" down here.)

I reminded her that her way of pounding up and down my stairs wasn't the passable way of navigating the staircase. Therefore, she needed to do it again. Typically, I got mouth, lip, attitude—whatever you want to call it. In the end, back up she went. It usually took a couple of times, because the first time or two, she would still be fairly peeved at the thought of having to walk up and down the stairs again.

This is where the consistency paid off. Having her walk back up the stairs one time was not going to do the trick if she stomped while doing it. She would need to walk up the stairs as many times as it took for her to do it without rattling the pictures on the walls.

It's all about respect. Did she respect me enough to listen to what I was telling her? If those pictures fell, I would be the one who had to clean up the mess and replace the frame and rehang the new picture. She had to understand that simply because she was upset about something, she didn't have the right to destroy the property that belonged to someone else.

Later, after she had successfully walked up the stairs and was in her room, I would go up and sit with her to reassure her that I loved her, and we would talk about what was bothering her. Whatever the discipline, the bottom line is the love behind it. It's easy to give them what they want. It's easy to be the fun parent all the time. It's easy to mistake that for love. Love is actually keeping them safe. Remember: A fish out of water will not be able to breathe indefinitely.

Respect is paramount at our house. It ought to be paramount everywhere, although from my vantage point, lack of respect seems to be a better fit. Kids, and especially older kids and teenagers, have little to no respect for others or other people's property. My children have been guilty of this at times too.

One afternoon, I received a phone call from Elliott's teacher. I could handle phone calls from the nurse. Those meant someone was sick or hurt. But a phone call from the teacher? That was a different matter entirely. Elliott is my baby. He is the youngest. He is probably one of the brightest kids I know, and most of the time, he is the sweetest of my three kiddos. So when his teacher called to tell me he had just come from a little visit to the principal's office for behavior, needless to say, I was stunned into silence.

Once I found my voice, I asked her if she was sure it was Elliott. She laughed and assured me that she had indeed sent the right child to the office. He had been busted for throwing wet paper towels up against the bathroom wall and watching them stick during a bathroom break. Honestly, I was relieved it wasn't something worse. She said he was downright devastated at having to go to the principal's office. I'm sure he was.

I promised her that he would be reprimanded at home. After all, it had been some time since we had needed to use the hot pokers or the rack. She laughed again, thanked me, and said, "Just thought you'd want to know."

Boy, did I ever. I'm totally sure that throwing wet paper towels up against the bathroom wall was great fun during a bathroom break, especially knowing your teacher was a girl and couldn't come into the boys' bathroom. Safe bet for some free playtime, right? Wrong. The vice principal's office (who just so happened to be a boy) was next door to said bathroom. Oops. Seven-year-olds don't think about that.

I told you I come from an "old school" background, which means I got spanked growing up. As a kid, I spent a lot of time with my great-grandmother. She had a paddle she named "Put Me to Work," and when I was about Elliott's age, I became very familiar with it. I'm a firm believer that a swat on the backside makes a child's ears open up. At the same time, I'm a firm believer that the punishment needs to fit the crime. I didn't figure taking a page out of my great-grandmother's book was the best plan right then.

Instead, I'd show Elliott the "proper" way to use a paper towel. That afternoon after school, he cleaned the upstairs bathroom. He wiped down the counter and cleaned the mirror, complaining the entire time. I stood right beside him, letting him know that he missed a spot. When I was comfortable with the state of the bathroom, I had him sit down and write his teacher a letter apologizing for his behavior, signed with the promise that he would never, ever do it again. He never had to clean the upstairs bathroom again. But Ethan? Well, that's another story.

I'm not a huge fan of cleaning my house, but it's a necessary evil. I would love to have someone do it for me, but alas, the task falls to me. Because I don't like to live in squalor, I must cowboy up, as the saying goes, grab my rubber gloves and a bottle of Scrubbing Bubbles, and get to work. The best time to clean my house is while the children are at school. The house is empty, there are precious few distractions, and I can get the job done quickly.

It takes the entire school day, but when I'm finished, my house looks amazing. The floors no longer bear sticky footprints of dripped ice cream and muddy paw prints. The bathrooms smell pine fresh. And the beds have clean sheets. The kids know beyond a shadow of a doubt which days are "cleaning days." The whole house smells like a Pine Sol factory—for at least thirty minutes after their arrival. Then everything returns to the way it was before.

One particular week during elementary school, all the kids were sick. Not bad sick, but congested sick: coughing, runny noses. I had been running vaporizers in their rooms at night to help with the coughing. I'd refill them as I put the kids to bed. For the best possible steam, you need to empty the old water and put new water in. One night, I carried the first vaporizer to the bathtub and was about to pour out the old water when I looked into the tub and found the biggest mess I had seen in a long time.

Someone had squirted hair conditioner up the wall and all across half the tub. From the looks of things, the culprit had been sitting on the toilet and the conditioner (which I buy in a large pump dispenser for Emma) was still sitting in the corner of the tub. It was time for a family meeting in the bathroom. Someone needed to be held accountable.

I called all three kids into the bathroom, pointed to the tub, and said, "Well?"

One said "Not me," another said "Oh, gross!" and the last one, eyes averted, was looking anywhere but at the tub or at me. There was my offender. I just love my Mom Radar. It comes standard with every positive pregnancy test. You do get to upgrade the frequency of your Mom Radar Operating System free with every kid and with every one of your oldest kiddo's birthdays. New operating systems come out each year. At the time of this event, I was working off MROS-9 (Mom Radar Operating System 9).

"Uh, Ethan, is there anything you want to tell me?"

The other two seemed to be glued to their spots. I think they would have been passing out popcorn to each other if they had had any. But I cut their fun short. "You two can go. Ethan?"

Emma and Elliott moved toward the door, but under their breath, I heard, "How does she *know*?"

Come to find out, he was, in fact, sitting on the throne, and he was bored. Guess I needed to put his Lego magazines in there. He told me he pushed the pump just "to see what it would do."

"For starters," I said, "it's a pump, so I'm guessing it was going to pump."

"Yeah, it did. And I thought it was cool. So I pushed it again and again and again. Then I kinda made a mess."

His plan was to clean it out when he took a shower that night, but surprise! No shower that night. Once again, I thought of my great-grandmother's paddle. I needed to pick my battles strategically, and conditioner in the bathtub wasn't a hill to die on. Instead, I told him to go downstairs and ask Daddy for the Comet bathroom cleaner and a clean rag. Then my honor roll student looked at me and asked, "Why?"

I just smiled.

When he came back upstairs, I explained how to clean a bathtub. I was especially put out because I had just cleaned the stupid thing not four hours earlier. Again, this discipline goes back to a safety issue. Conditioner is slippery. The first kid to climb into that bathtub would have busted his or her little tooshie. I told him to rinse out all the conditioner.

He said "Finished" and made like he was going to leave the bathroom.

"Wrong, chief."

I showed him how to sprinkle the powder, and he said, "Oh my goodness, this smells terrible. Mom, *seriously*." Gasp, cough, choke. I—can't—breathe." (Evidently, Emma isn't the only one with drama skills.)

Since he was left with no option but to complete the cleanup, he pulled his shirt up over his nose, occasionally turning his head away from the tub, pulling down his shirt so he could take a big breath, and then getting back to work wiping out the inside of the tub.

"MOM!" Gasp, cough, choke. "How much longer?"

I showed him how to rinse, trying so hard not to laugh.

"Mom, really. Why are you making me do this? Didn't you just do this?" Gasp, cough, choke.

Thank you, son. It was the perfect opportunity to explain to him that, yes, I had just done this, but he had chosen to ruin the work I had done. This foul-smelling (which doesn't smell that bad) cleaner he couldn't stand was what I'd used to clean the bathtub. He carelessly chose to squirt conditioner all over the tub, making it unsafe for anyone to use. This was a boundary I was setting for him. One he would not soon forget. Kids need boundaries.

Have you ever seen those antiquated, wire-and-pole electric fences used in backyards for puppies? A puppy or even a grown dog will test its boundaries every now and then to see if there are any weak spots. They won't do it all the time or even every day, just from time to time.

It's the same with kids and their boundaries. No, I'm not suggesting that you use electric fences on your children! (I can see the headlines now: "Woman Tells Readers to Use Duct Tape and Electric Fences for Discipline.")

I have great kids. They're obedient, contrary to the last couple of stories. I can send them to their friends' houses for dinners and sleepovers and know that I will hear about their good manners and good behavior.

But every now and then, they test their "fence." When they do, you must be ready with your follow-through! Do not spout empty threats. If you say you're going to do something, think like Nike and JUST DO IT! They know when you're bluffing.

Case in point: When our kids were seven, eight, and nine, we found ourselves at Disney World again for spring break. (Apparently, we didn't learn the first time we were there with the multitudes.) We drove this time—and we were sans babysitter. Because the kids were older, we thought we could handle it. Famous last words.

The parks had more people in them than I ever thought possible. I googled "max attendance" just to get a ballpark figure. I swear the number was off by at least twenty-five thousand. There were wall-to-wall people, and we were right in the middle.

Since we had been there before, the kids had their own ideas about which ride to go on next and how to use the FastPass, and, above anything else, how boring Mom and Dad were. Well, I got a little nervous being stuck in the middle of a crowd of close to one hundred thousand people while my kids ran in three different directions. I'd just about had enough of Ethan and Elliott bolting from me when I corralled them all and shouted above the noise, "If anyone else runs away from me, I'm calling the hotel and getting a sitter for y'all, and Daddy and I will come back to Disney without you!"

Ethan looked me square in the eye. "You would not."

I stood straight up. "Try me."

Ten minutes later, he was gone again. He wanted to do Splash Mountain. None of us were all that fired up about getting wet again, so we said no. But he didn't care.

It took a long minute to find him. We didn't know which direction he had gone. Splash Mountain was one way at a fork, and we were headed down the other side. I was close to panicking. That alone would have probably taught him a lesson because we had been separated long enough to scare him. The only trouble with leaving it at that lesson was my warning to all three kids that if anyone ran off again, I would get them a sitter. Ethan ran off, so I called the hotel.

Jeff's jaw hit the ground. He couldn't believe I actually did that. Our hotel was part of one of the largest and best-known hotel chains in the world—five stars and the whole nine yards. I figured we couldn't be the only parents who needed a slight break from their kids. Turns out, we weren't. They had a Mary Poppins wannabe ready for us in a matter of hours.

We left the park and drove back to our hotel. The kids sat in stunned silence the whole time. Although it was Ethan's choice to run toward Splash Mountain—the straw that broke the camel's back—all three children were guilty of unsupervised excursions throughout the Magic Kingdom. So my decision to return all of them to the hotel was justified.

Remember, this is about the follow-through. I laid the ground rules: If a certain action happened again, there would be an opposite and swift reaction from me. The children clearly didn't believe me, but when they tested the strength of their electric fence, they didn't find a weak spot. Instead, they found all circuits fully functional and wired hot.

A side note: The woman the hotel sent to us was, in fact, Mary Poppins's double. She had a bag full of tricks, complete with games, crafts, and who knows what else. When we got back to the hotel that night, the table was filled with twenty or so pictures and crafts the children had made. I guess I should have told her she was a punishment! The next morning, the kids asked when Miss Betty could come back.

We tend to mix and match things from our past with things from our present to try to make sense of our lives for our future. I've reared my kids mostly based on the way I was reared. My parents and my extended family did a good job with me. My husband has the same train of thought. We're on the same page. That's important not only for raising your children—but for keeping your family and marriage intact and healthy.

Very few things will drive a wedge faster and further between a husband and wife than disagreements about how to discipline children. Before we got married, Jeff and I talked about seemingly little things. We would laugh and joke about getting grounded when we were kids. We discussed whether or not we got spanked, to which we both replied, "Yep." We had similar experiences with school versus home. When we got in trouble at school, there was going to be more waiting at home.

Those memories made us both smile. Not because we are gluttons for punishment. Our parents didn't beat us. We weren't abused children. Our parents knew what was going on in our world. My mother talked to my teachers. She was involved. I'm the oldest of four girls. Mother had to be involved. Jeff's folks did the same thing. I understand that for some of you reading this book, you and your spouse come from different backgrounds. That does make things more challenging—but it does *not* make them impossible.

When two people get married, they get to start fresh. They leave their parents' house and cleave to each other. That means they stick together. When you get married, you begin to form your own new family unit with new traditions, new rules, and a new game plan. You don't discount the way you were brought up, but you weave your past—*both* your pasts—into your future. Everyone will have something new to tell you and some new way of doing things. Look at me! That's what I'm doing. I'm telling you what has worked for us. It can work for you too, at least most days.

My kids, cute as they are, are still kids. And they will be the first to tell you that it's super fun to feed a fish, but when you feed Flippy too much, he explodes.

7.

You Shoved *What* Up Your Nose?

When kids run in and around and through your house, one of them will inevitably get hurt. Hopefully the injuries are minor, and all you'll have to do is pull some frozen peas from the freezer or perhaps visit your local pharmacy or pediatrician. But once in a while, kids will pull a stunt requiring a fast trip to a specialist's office or the mother ship—otherwise known as the emergency room.

Do you remember the TV show *Everybody Loves Raymond*? Well, contrary to popular belief, not everybody loves Raymond. I happen to love Raymond—well, actually, Marie (Ray's mom)—but my children don't love anyone from the show. In fact, when we go surfing through the channels and I happen to land on *Raymond*, the moans and wails that come spouting from my children can only be compared to the wailing and gnashing of teeth you might find at the biblical end of days. "Not Raymond! I don't *love* Raymond!"

In one particular episode, Marie showcases her skill as a human thermometer. I got the biggest kick out of that episode. Marie can tell by touch if someone has a fever, and if so, what that fever is right down to the decimal. She does this by kissing the person's forehead. It just so happens that Debra, Ray's wife, comes down with the fever, so she becomes the recipient of Marie's red lipstick lip prints all over her forehead. This is an ability that has been given to mothers everywhere. It utterly astounds my husband.

When I ran away from home a few years ago and was enjoying my seat on a westbound plane bound for California to catch up on some much-needed rest and relaxation, I left all three of my children in the care of their father. I was comfortable in my decision not to call in the cavalry (my mother-in-law). Jeff was competent enough to handle the homework, the lunches, the bedtimes, the breakfasts, and even the dinners. I had high hopes that teeth would be brushed a couple of times over the course of the week I was gone and that baths would also be administered at least twice.

What I didn't count on was a phone call from my daughter four days into my trip. This is where you rethink teaching your children your cell phone number. Here's what our conversation sounded like:

Me: Hello?

Emma: Mom? When are you coming home?

Me: Not for a few more days. Why? Is everything okay? Where's Daddy?

Emma: He's in his office. We don't feel very good.

Me (stomach does a backflip): What do you mean "we"? Where are your brothers? What doesn't feel good?

Emma: The boys are here. We're coughing. And we feel . . . we just don't . . . feel good.

Me: What does Daddy say?

Emma: He said we were fine. We needed to go to bed and go to sleep.

Me: Put Daddy on the phone.

From California, there wasn't much I could do. I couldn't lean over and kiss them to see who had a fever and who didn't. I couldn't listen effectively to their cough to discern who needed the doctor and who needed Benadryl. My husband, bless his heart, comes from the school of thought that eventually your body will heal itself. And when you're forty, perhaps that works. But when you're a little kid—I don't buy that particular line of garbage.

I came home from California three days later to three kids with sinus infections, two of whom had bronchitis to boot and one had croup. Ten days' worth of antibiotics later, and all three were right as rain. (Mom Radar alert: There is a reason we are the moms. MROS-20! Upgrade yours today!)

I didn't always have the latest version of the Mom Radar. Lucky for me, my kids have always tested me on whichever version I was running.

My boys have asthmatic tendencies. They don't have full-blown asthma, but when they do get something like bronchitis, they wheeze with gusto. It was bad enough that we purchased our very own nebulizer machine so we could administer breathing treatments whenever necessary.

When the boys were babies, this happened *all the time*. It seemed they were constantly sick. I kept adding a new kid to the mix every year, so I was at the doctor's office every other week for something. I was there for shots for one kid, sick visit for another, or an ear recheck for still another. It was during one of those visits when my pediatrician mentioned to me that she thought both Ethan and Emma would benefit greatly from having ear tubes put in. Emma was six months old, Ethan was twenty months old, and I was pregnant with Elliott. Between the two of them, we had had seventeen ear infections in the house. It was time for tubes.

She recommended a wonderful ear, nose, and throat doctor—Dr. Chan—who saw the kids and scheduled them for surgery. The very next day, my doctor put me in a different hospital for extreme dehydration. He would keep me there for a week and some change. Jeff had to handle the ear tube surgery without me.

Now, before y'all get too worried about him, he had *his* momma with him. Nana was not about to let him fly completely solo on this gig. She was there to do the heavy lifting. Those babies came out of anesthesia fighting like tigers, from what I understand, and Nana was the only one who could have controlled them. There is a magical peace that comes from the arms of the Nanas and the Grannies. Maybe it's because they have already lived through episodes like this. Or maybe it's because they know they get to give these fighting kids back to their parents and walk away. Who knows?

All I do know is that on that day we couldn't have done it without her. Thankfully, those ear tubes worked like a charm, and the ear infections disappeared. Sweet as our Dr. Chan was and as well as the tubes worked, that would not be the last we saw of him.

I'm convinced that children are really super-cute carrier monkeys. Their job is to pick up and attract the latest and greatest germ, bug, or virus and bring it home to share with the rest of the family. We teach our children to share, but we fail miserably to distinguish between the germs and the good stuff. Having three kids in twenty-six months was pretty close to having twins with a spare, so they passed everything back and forth to one another.

The most memorable thing we passed around was a particularly nasty piece of work known as the rotavirus. A few years back, doctors tried to develop a vaccine for it, but then decided the vaccine was worse than actual virus, which blows my mind because having lived through the virus, I can't imagine anything worse.

It was Easter weekend and I was pregnant with Elliott. Ethan wasn't feeling well. He had had some sort of tummy bug, and it was coming out the diapered end, but not coming from the top end. Emma seemed to be in good shape. Praises to the Lord on that one. I felt miserable, but that's how I always felt when I was pregnant. If my eyes were open, I was throwing up—I mean "glowing."

Jeff and I packed up the kids and headed to Austin for the holiday. This was before my parents lost their minds and caught the wanderlust bug to hit the open road on their quest to find America. During the two-and-a-half-hour drive, Ethan kept getting worse—the diarrhea got more and more volatile—and then Emma seemed to be a bit lethargic. I felt really miserable, but again, I didn't think too much of that.

Once we got to Austin, all three of us could do nothing but lie around and let my mother—Granny—take care of us. For an added bonus, I wasn't the only one throwing up; Ethan and Emma started throwing up as well. Jeff was fine—so far.

In situations like this, it's imperative to keep fluids in little bodies. Any type of fluid. Doctors will tell you Pedialyte. That stuff tastes terrible. I mixed Sprite with water, and they liked that. When you have kids running a fever and throwing up everything but their toenails, you've got to keep fluids in them. Watered-down Coke or Sprite is the best. It worked for us when were kids, and it will do the same for your kids. We munched on saltine crackers and prayed that God would just let us die.

By Easter Sunday, we felt a little better, good enough to head to my grandparent's house for lunch. We didn't make it to church—they don't have couches for us to lie on in the sanctuary. We should have driven straight home to Houston because by going to Leander (a little town just outside of Austin), we contaminated my *entire* family: my grandmother, my grandfather, my great-grandmother, two aunts, two uncles, two cousins, not to mention both my parents and all three sisters. I didn't think they would ever let us come back to visit after that one.

The rotavirus is like the stomach flu on steroids. It lasted for two weeks. Although it did progressively get less and less virulent, it was still horrible to the nth degree. I fed the kids a lot of bananas, yogurt, and applesauce during that time. If you can avoid the rota, do so! Oh, yeah, Jeff eventually got it too.

No one can escape it.

I was also ill-prepared for the really weird baby diseases like mad cow or hoof-and-mouth (although technically, those aren't the exact names for them.) The kids—well, one kid (who can remember which one?)—came home with something called hand-foot-and-mouth disease, which I promptly also forgot the name of, so I switched it to hoof-and-mouth. As I was explaining this to my mother, she thought it was mad cow, and so the story goes.

HFM (hand-foot-and-mouth) starts with a fever. After that's gone, a rash appears inside the mouth that looks like little blisters or ulcers. It really drove the kids nuts. I felt bad for them. The rash can also show up on the palms of their hands or the soles of their feet, hence the name. Anyone can get HFM, but it usually affects infants and children under the age of ten.

The kids had it three times. Oh joy. But don't freak out (as I did) if it visits you. It doesn't mean you're dirty or need a lesson in personal hygiene, even though that was my first thought. I'm here to tell you that kids pick up germs everywhere! They are a magnet for them. And it doesn't help that their favorite way to learn about something is to *put it into their mouth.* And all God's sisters said, "Gross!"

Once Elliott arrived, that pretty much secured me a front-row parking spot at the pediatrician's office. I was there every week. It brought me closer to my pediatrician, who is now one of my very good friends. Our families have even vacationed to Disney World together. When Ethan had tubes put in his ears, we thought that would fix most of his major ailments. But as the old saying goes, that's what you get for thinking. I told you we hadn't seen the last of Dr. Chan, our ENT.

Each time the winds of change blew through the great city of Houston, they kicked up new pollutants, new pollen spores, and new sources of gunk that sent Ethan's immune system into a literal tailspin. We were quite familiar with both bronchitis and pneumonia. Imagine my surprise when my pediatrician suggested that Ethan have his tonsils removed.

We had dealt with everything else: upper respiratory infections, sinus infections, and every level of bronchitis. But we had escaped strep throat. I was wracking my brain. I could think of only one time—and that was a big maybe—that we'd had the dubious pleasure of having strep in the house. I thought multiple cases of strep throat were the major reason kids had their tonsils removed.

Well, not exactly.

Do you know the tonsils' primary function? Don't worry, neither did I. Let me tell you. Their job is to trap all the germs that come into your body through your mouth and nose and then dispose of them. The problem occurs when the garbage coming in presents too much of a workload for the tonsils. They still trap everything, but once they get overloaded, they simply hold onto it rather than disposing of it. And then they grow and grow and grow.

That's where we were with five-year-old Ethan. Tonsils are located on either side of the throat and shouldn't touch. His tonsils were so enlarged with yuckiness that they were kissing. They were no longer getting rid of the junk—they were hoarding it. It was time for them to go.

The surgery for removing tonsils and adenoids, an extension of the tonsils, is fairly routine. That's what I would have told anyone whose child was going in for this operation. That's what people told me. I am here to tell you, statistics do not mean jack when it's your kid going under the knife. A tonsillectomy doesn't take very long to perform. But the waiting can be excruciating. My imagination ran wild with thoughts of what he was going through: Would the doctor do a good job? Were the nurses qualified to take care of him before he was fully asleep?

Another little nugget of advice to any parent whose child will undergo surgery: Hit the gym every day for a couple of weeks *before* your child's big day. If your kiddos are like any of mine, they will wake up from anesthesia swinging for the fence. You'll need all the extra strength you can muster to fight them off!

When you watch TV and you see people waking up from surgery, they seem disoriented and groggy, but otherwise fine. Y'all, that is staged for TV. If you ever see children doing that, they are made of plastic! Jeff and I were sitting in the waiting room blindly flipping through magazines when a nurse came out to get us. We thought it was pretty fast, but that was all we had time to think about. As soon as we passed through the double doors she had exited, we heard it: a scream like something from a caged wild animal, low and guttural.

Somebody's not having a very good day, I thought. We walked through another door, and the sound grew more frantic and louder. The nurses were looking at us intensely now. My heart started racing as we walked through the last door and headed for a secluded room past the rows of children who were sitting up in their beds eating Popsicles. None of them were screaming.

I looked through the window of this little room and saw a child possessed and two nurses distraught. Ethan was in a full breach, arms spread wide, mouth wide open, trying desperately to escape the death grip the nurses had on him. His eyes were closed. I doubt his legs would have supported him had he tried to stand.

I threw open the door and grabbed him. He calmed immediately. I sank into a chair. Truth be told, I almost fainted. He was still attached to his IV, he was scared, and he was hurting. The worst part: It was only the beginning.

After a tonsillectomy, you can expect your kiddo to be down for three or four days, a week at most. Kids are manufactured by Rubbermaid. They bounce back with exceptional speed.

That was *not* the case with Ethan. After four days of lying on the couch and not eating much, he still wasn't up and around. Knowing that my kids leaned a bit toward the dramatic side of life, I honestly thought he was milking the whole "I just had surgery, pity me" thing. I was wrong.

Somewhere around a week after his surgery, he told me that one of his legs hurt. Odd. The kid had his tonsils taken out, and his legs were a ways away from his throat. Being filled with kindness and compassion and having a four-year-old and a three-year-old running through the house, I told him his leg hurt because he hadn't used it in a week and that he needed to get up and move around.

He was supremely obedient in those days, so he slowly swung his legs over the side of the couch, tried to stand up, and quickly hit the ground. His legs simply wouldn't support him. He began to cry. I became concerned. I picked him up, put him back on the couch, and took a good look at him. His left leg, from the knee down, was swollen, and purple dots were emerging all over both legs. This couldn't be good.

Before Jeff got home from work, Ethan's legs had started to swell, along with his elbows and his hands. They were tender to the touch. I was trying to comfort him without showing how worried I was.

Twenty-four hours later, there was no change, so we drove to the ER.

We got in right away, and the ER doctor was brilliant. We told her he had his tonsils taken out about a week earlier. The dawn of understanding spread wide across her face. Here's the skinny on what happened in a nutshell: Ethan's tonsils were so full of nastiness that the first cut to take them out flooded his little body with toxins. His immune system—which was already taxed because the tonsils were hoarding germs, not destroying them—bailed on him. His body was shutting down against this onslaught of poison coursing through it.

Bottom line: There was nothing we could do. The purple spots came from his blood vessels, which were leaking. Blood was in his stool because the blood vessels in his kidneys were leaking, along with the blood vessels in the lining of his stomach. There is no medication for this. Let me say that again: *There is no medication for this.* You wait it out. You pray.

This disorder is called Henoch-Schonlein purpura. I have never been so afraid in my life.

Over the next six weeks (because that's how long it took for this horrible ailment to "run its course"), I did some major bartering with God: begging, pleading, whatever you want to call it. Only God's grace and mercy could keep those toxins from attacking the blood vessels in Ethan's heart or his brain. If the toxins went to either organ, we would lose him. We needed a miracle. This "reaction" happens to one in about five hundred thousand kids. But as I said earlier, statistics don't mean jack when it's your kid.

Spending a month and a half at home with Ethan took its toll on me. I followed him around constantly. I was so afraid he would need something. Or that he would fall down. He was a little bitty thing before his surgery, and then after it—my word! He lost almost ten pounds. I could pick him up and carry him around in one arm. He didn't have any strength. He drank a lot of those Boost drinks for kids. I mixed them with ice cream and made little shakes for him. He was my easy kid. I was thankful—especially the afternoon I got a phone call from the preschool.

Me: Hello?

Office: Dallas, we need you to come and get Elliott.

Me: Is he okay?

Office: Yes, but he shoved a playground rock up his nose. I can't reach it. He's freaking out. We need you to come get him.

Me: Terrific. I'm on my way.

Every house has that *one* kid. Elliott is my *one*. Although in light of the last story, you would think Ethan is my one. Nope. It's Elliott. The thing about playground rocks is this: They're little, so they fit up a nose. They also fit into ears, although with ears, they usually pop right out. Noses are a different story completely. Two reasons: (1) You can push them up with your finger as (2) you suck in with your breath. Both of these actions, when combined, create the problem.

So I had to go get Elliott while calling Dr. Chan's office for an emergency appointment to remove a playground rock. It's a good thing I don't mind being the center of attention because as I was hanging up with the nurse at his office, I could hear them laughing.

Unfortunately, we didn't make it to the office before the rock made the turn from the bridge of the nose into no-man's-land. I guess the urge to sniff was too great for Elliott to resist. Another good thing about playground rocks is their small size. What goes up and in must come down and out.

For those who may not be as well acquainted with the anatomy of nasal passages as I had to become, let me explain. Most of the time, if you can suck something up through your nose, you can also swallow it down your throat and into your tummy, where it will eventually follow the same pathway as food to leave the body.

That concludes today's anatomy lesson. You are most welcome.

• • •

It was little more than a year after Ethan's surgery and subsequent very long recovery that I found myself sitting in my pediatrician's office with Elliott, listening to her hand me yet another pneumonia diagnosis for him. She recommended Elliott have his tonsils removed as well. You can just imagine how fired up I was about that. She had to do some pretty smooth talking and super convincing to assure me that Elliott's surgery would go much better.

Elliott was a year younger than Ethan at the time of his surgery, and he would also be having his sinuses scraped. Ick. Thankfully, Elliott was the poster child for the recovery—except for right after the operation. He, too, came out of anesthesia fighting like a tiger. I was beginning to think they saved this isolation room just for us.

In the first few days, I watched him like a hawk, sure that purple dots would emerge and his appendages would swell. Nothing happened. He was back to his usual self in no time and wanted to play, not understanding why he couldn't run around. I had to fight to keep him at home and on the couch. When I finally felt comfortable enough to send him to school, he was all smiles and raring to go.

Because Elliott's surgery was more involved than his brother's, his operation lasted longer. He came into recovery looking like Hannibal Lector. His nose was packed with gauze, and he had a drip pad taped under his nose. Ugh! I'm getting queasy just thinking about it. Doing a sinus scrape on a set of little sinuses is tedious and slow going.

A couple of weeks after surgery, the doc wanted to take a look. Think about this for a minute: Where are your sinuses? Under your eyes and *up your nose*, right? How do you suppose the doc is going to get a peek up there? Doctors have fabulous little tools and toys. Dr. Chan is no exception. He had this long, skinny scope he was going to use to look up Elliott's nose to make sure the stitches were dissolving and everything was moving right along.

Let's pause for a second.

If you have never taken your child to a doctor who does not have children, I highly recommend that you try one out at least once. They are so much fun to mess with! Y'all, I am not a doctor. At the time of Elliott's follow-up appointment, I had no idea what this man was about to attempt with my son. If I had caught on a little sooner, I would have suggested something or someone a little sturdier than I am to use as the only means of restraint.

So I was sitting in this chair with Elliott on my lap, and Dr. Chan said, "Okay, Mom. I'm going to need you to give him a good hug while I look up his nose."

It was laughable. He started coming at Elliott with this skinny little scope that was about the width and length of a pipe cleaner while I was trying desperately to get Elliott into a pretzel hold—which was so not working. As he tried to push Elliott's head back to put the scope up his nose, Elliott got one hand loose, grabbed the scope, and made his own pretzel. All movement from all parties involved stopped immediately. Dr. Chan looked at me, stood up, and excused himself from the exam room.

There's something you need to know about our ENT. Yes, he's Asian, as evidenced by his name. He is one of the best in Houston and also one of the most mild-mannered men I have ever met. Standing somewhere around six feet tall, he wears ostrich skin cowboy boots with his scrubs. His IQ hovers just above brilliant, yet he relates well to both adults and children.

But when Elliott snapped his scope, I swear smoke came out of the man's ears. It took fifteen minutes for him to come back into the room with us. He managed a quick look in Elliott's throat and his ears—and wisely left his nose alone.

Then the nurse came in to check us out. I apologized profusely. She smiled sweetly and said, "Wow. Didn't know that scope could bend like that. You'd think for four thousand dollars, it'd be a little bit stronger."

I told you, Elliott is my *one*. Four grand—gone in four seconds. Awesome.

8.

Motrin, Xanax, and Other Drugs

Having doctors as friends comes in handy, especially when you have a kid like Elliott. By the age of seven, he had had three concussions and broken his nose at least once—the jury is still out on the second time. Granted, the concussions had all been mild, but a head injury is a head injury. The kid had no fear! He still has no fear. I have enough fear for the both of us, and soon you'll see why. He has had three CAT scans, and I've lost count on the chest X-rays. Suffice it to say, if he undergoes any more radiation, we can use him for a power source the next time a hurricane blows through Houston.

One of the times he decided to tear himself up was, thankfully, in front of my pediatrician. She has three kids almost the same age as mine, lined up in the same order—boy, girl, boy—although hers are spaced just a bit further apart than mine. One summer day they came over to swim, and everyone was having a good time. Then four-year-old Elliott raced around the corner of the patio. He turned to look over his shoulder, tripped over his own feet, and smacked his head—face-first—into the bottom step of the hot tub. Blood, big knot, lots of tears. The whole nine yards. Not to mention five other kids rushing to see what had happened.

The force of the blow broke the cartilage across his nose. And he got a mild concussion from slamming his forehead into the hard flagstone step. All I can say is I'm glad I had a witness. Elliott was forever doing stuff like that. And every time he did, I spent two nights on the floor beside his bed, waking him up every couple of hours:

"Ellie, what's your name?"

"Elliott."

"What's my name?"

"Mommy."

"What's my other name?"

"Dallas."

The last chapter was filled with strange childhood diseases—this one is a glimpse into my own personal Child Protective Services file. Just kidding! I don't really have one—but there for a while, I thought they would come knocking at any moment.

My children had the privilege of going to a parochial school (preschool through high school). For my husband and me, it meant they got individual attention and an education based on the beliefs and foundation of the Bible. For our children, it meant they couldn't ride a big yellow school bus, so they were always car riders.

One day, I was walking out the door to pick them up when the phone rang. It was the school. I thought about not answering. The day was almost over. Then again, whatever it was had to be bad enough that it couldn't wait fifteen minutes until the final bell.

Office: Hi, Dallas, this is Nurse Jane.

Me: Hey. Who do you have?

Office: Ethan. I don't want to worry you, but he took a pretty good blow to the head—

Me: He *what*?

Office: Well, he was on the pavilion at recess, playing kickball, and as he was sliding into home, he misjudged the distance and hit the fence. He's okay. But he's bleeding pretty good.

Me: Does he need stitches?

Office: He might. We did have to change his shirt. You should probably have him looked at.

Me: Keep him with you. I'm on my way. I'm sending Jeff to get the other two.

When I saw Ethan, he had an ice pack over his left eye. He'd whacked his head on the fence and popped it open in the middle of an eyebrow. I called the pediatrician's office, described the situation, and said we were on our way. I didn't ask if they had time.

Ethan was super excited about not crying on the playground. He did tell me his stomach hurt a little when he saw all the blood, but he was very brave. Mom was brave too—until we got to the doctor's office.

Head injuries. They bleed and bleed and bleed. The other thing with head wounds is that if you ice them, they don't bleed as much, but as soon as you take the ice off—BAM!—you are back to full flow. On the drive to the doctor's office, Ethan didn't have the ice pack on his head anymore, so it had opened back up. Once we got inside the office and I could see the wound clearly, I got very queasy. As I've mentioned, I don't do well with blood. It isn't my forte. I do better with broken bones.

The nurses fixed him up with a new ice pack and took us to a room. He sat in a chair, holding the ice pack with one hand and flipping through a book with the other while I lay on the exam table trying to remember my Lamaze breathing in a vain attempt to remain calm. I thought he might be more traumatized if his mother passed out than from the actual injury itself. Plus, I didn't want Dr. Hanson to have to sew us both up. This would not be the last time Ethan had a bleeding head wound and I was the one lying down.

When Dr. Hanson walked into the room, she burst out laughing at the sight of me on the table and Ethan in the chair. She tried to compose herself. "Uh, Mom? You're going to have to get off the table. I need it for the patient."

I assured her I knew this, but she failed to understand that if I weren't on the table, she would quickly have two patients.

As excited as Ethan was in the beginning about getting stitches, when the rubber actually started to hit the road, he changed his mind. Maybe stitches weren't the way to go. Lucky for him, the doctor agreed. He needed glue. Superglue. Surgical superglue.

Faster than stitches but burns like fire. There was an upside: He did get to go to school with white tape over his eyebrow, and everyone knows that the chicks dig battle wounds.

In April of every year, my church has an annual family camping trip to a local state park. Sign-up sheets get passed around, and families converse back and forth about who's going, who wants to be placed next to whom, and so on. We signed up for the fun-filled annual event when the kids were eight, nine, and ten years old. Remember Nelson? We loaded him up and headed out.

When we arrived at the park, our kids were instantly drawn to this large ditch across the way from the campsites that played host to numerous fallen pine trees, hollow logs, and rocks. In short, it was a kid's dream come true. Also lying in the ditch was an old two-by-four that happened to be the perfect size for a swing. My husband, being the masterly engineer that he is, found a long rope and somehow managed to fashion a swing of sorts using this piece of wood and one of the trees. The kids (almost forty of them!) loved this setup. It seemed to be the ideal playground equipment.

About a day and a half into our three-day trip, we heard a

crescendo of screams of panic and pain coming from the ditch. Naturally, the adults nearby sprang into action. The bigger kids were among the first to make it to us.

"Ethan is hurt! He's hurt real bad!"

I swear my heart actually stopped.

When we saw Ethan walking toward the campground, I was so relieved to see he was still upright. He was crying, but from the front he looked okay. It wasn't until I got closer that I realized "okay" wasn't the proper word.

"My head! My head is open!" he screamed. "I'm going to die!"

When I checked the back of his head, I saw a silver-dollar-sized hole. I instinctively reached for the open wound to apply pressure to stop the copious amount of blood flowing from his head. It was an absolute miracle he was still on his feet. In between murmured words of comfort to him, I was shouting scathing words at the other children, demanding that someone tell me how this happened.

My line of fire landed on the poor child who caused the accident: William. Bless his heart. Almost as hysterical as Ethan, he told me that he was swinging back and forth (as all the kids had been doing over the last couple of days) when Ethan bent down to pick up a stick. As Ethan stood up, William and the swing collided with the back of Ethan's head, thus splitting the skin clean open and exposing the bone.

William honestly thought Ethan was going to die, and if he did, it would be all his fault. I did nothing to change his way of thinking. That was one of my lowest moments in parenting. It was an accident—a bloody and gruesome accident, but still an accident.

Do you have a sixth sense? I think I do. But only sometimes. Earlier that morning, as we were all sitting around drinking our coffee, during a lull in the conversation, I asked if anyone knew where the closest emergency room was. They all looked at me as if I had just sprouted pretty pink polka dots. At the time, it was a very random question. I explained that here we were, in the middle of nowhere, with close to forty kids—I figured someone was going to make a trip to the ER. I had no idea that in less than three hours' time, it would be us.

One of our friends, Lesli, grabbed a towel—my hand was doing an exceptionally poor job of stopping the blood flow—and hopped into the back seat of Jeff's truck with us, ready to make the thirty-mile trip to the Livingston Memorial Hospital. I'm pretty sure Jeff broke the sound barrier to get us there. It amazes me how well we react to a crisis. During the ride to the hospital, I was calm and collected, doing what I needed to do. I kept the pressure on Ethan's head. I talked to him and made sure he knew who he was and who I was.

But once we got to the hospital, all of my capabilities must have stayed in the truck. Signing him in at the registration desk, I could feel my knees getting weaker and weaker. As we walked back to the triage room, I got hotter and hotter, and you know how cold hospitals are. Ten minutes later, we were settled into an exam room. The nurse came in through the door, greeted Ethan, looked at me, and opened her mouth to speak, but Ethan beat her to it. "Uh, Mom . . . you don't look so good."

The nurse agreed. "Yeah Mom, we're gonna need you to get on the floor as fast as you can."

Too late.

My knees buckled and I was down. Jeff moved fast to make sure our sweet nurse didn't have two head wounds to sew up. That's about the time Lesli came back into the room. She had stepped out to make a quick phone call to the camp. The sight that greeted her was almost comical. Ethan was sitting on the exam table, I was on the floor with the nurse, and Jeff was huddled over me. Evidently, my adrenaline stopped once I turned Ethan over to the hospital staff. I was fine, just a little too woozy to be on my feet. We all thought it best if I stayed on the floor.

Ethan was such a trooper! He got four staples in the back of his head and a swell V-shaped scar. He was totally pumped about the scar. I think it has to be a boy thing. Come to think of it, Jeff is very proud of all his scars too.

We left the hospital with an ice pack for Ethan's head, an ice pack for me (should I get light-headed again), two Xanax to chill me out a tad, and memories for a lifetime. Two and a half weeks later, the staples came out. The scar is still there—right smack-dab in the middle of the back of his head. Our pediatrician was not especially thrilled with the backwoods patch job on Ethan's head, though. While the four staples did close the hole in his head, the wound, according to her, actually required *ten* staples.

Not to be outdone by his big brother, Elliott upped his game. I told you, he is my one. He will try anything. He will jump, dive, or climb off or over any structure or cliff or rock you put in his path.

About a month after Ethan started looking like a Revolutionary War soldier (due to the exceptional head bandage), I received yet another phone call from the school nurse. Caller ID is a wonderful thing. Anytime the school's name and number popped up in my window, I paused a second and pondered which kid would most likely be in her office.

I happened to be on campus when she called. "Hey, Dallas," she said, "we think Elliott broke his arm. We need you to come get him."

Here we were, within four short weeks of dealing with a wide-open, blood-gushing head wound, and now a broken arm. (The next book I write will be an exposé on the top ten hospitals of East Texas!)

I ran to the nurse's office and found Elliott cradled by the school secretary, his arm iced and splinted, crocodile tears in his eyes, waiting for me to get him. Poor little guy.

How did all of this go down? He and his friends were playing a game at recess. Elliott was evading capture from the enemies, who incidentally were throwing fireballs at him, and he did his best *Mission Impossible* vault over the side of the highest slide on the playground, landing in perfect push-up position, cracking his right radius. Awesome.

So another visit to the emergency room. Twenty-four hours later, Elliott was the proud owner of a royal blue, waterproof cast. I'd love to say that was the end of our emergency room visits, but given my kids—especially my boys—that's laughable.

I had a daredevil bucking to be the next Evel Knievel and God only knew what Ethan would do next. Emma, on the other hand, was different from her brothers—in the early years. She didn't try to skydive off the roof and or jump curbs on her bike. Boys are very active. They just go. They just do.

Emma did mattress-surf down the stairs, thanks to the Princess Diaries movies. But I could live with that, though she confessed that she wanted to break something, preferably her leg. She wanted crutches so she could duct-tape them in pretty fashionable colors and figured she needed to break a leg to get them. I was almost certain she was devising a plan to make it happen. Lucky for her, I special ordered a large quantity of Bubble Wrap from eBay to wrap her in it to keep her extra safe.

Turns out, it wasn't her legs that needed the extra protection but her wrists.

Emma loved watching the Summer Olympics. I enjoyed them

growing up too. Mary Lou Retton was the coolest person in the world when I was a kid. I remember watching her and thinking, *I want to be just like her.* Of course I also wanted to be a ballerina, an astronaut, a princess, and a teacher. Currently, I am none of those things. But I thought about them.

So during the 2012 Summer Olympics in London, it didn't surprise me in the least when nine-year-old Emma decided that she, too, had been bitten by the gymnastics bug. We watched all the routines. We cheered on Team USA. We even recorded the events so she could watch them over and over again. Her train of thought was simple: *How hard can this be?*

Harder than you think.

As I explained earlier, our open floor plan allows me to hear almost everything that goes on upstairs from any room downstairs—including a tumbling little girl trying to duplicate floor routines from the Team USA gymnastics squad. I knew when my child did or did not stick her landing. During one of her attempts, she fell. She assured me she was fine.

Two days later, my extremely left-handed child was eating with her right hand, trying to do homework with her right hand, and brushing her teeth with her right hand. The diagnosis? A broken left wrist. The cause? An attempted reenactment of Aly Raisman's gold medal floor routine when she danced to "Hava Nagila."

The following January, it was Elliott's turn again.

In our house, and I would wager in most houses, we had a few basic rules. One was DON'T RUN. Elliott never understood this rule. He couldn't hear it when I told him. He couldn't read it when I wrote it down. Running was like air to this child.

One afternoon I called him downstairs. Naturally, the only

acceptable means of appearing to my summons was to sprint at full speed. Looking back at this event now, I'm thankful he didn't slide down the stairs on his head.

As he bolted out of his room, ran through the playroom, and jumped the two little steps from the playroom onto the landing at the top of the stairs, he, like his sister a couple of months earlier—did not stick his landing. His right leg crumpled underneath him, cracking just above the growth plate on his right ankle.

Needless to say, Emma was very disappointed that Elliott would be the first to receive the crutches.

Honestly, I was afraid to call our orthopedic. In the time span of *less than* one year, we had a major head wound, a broken arm, a broken wrist, and now a broken leg. At this point, I was expecting Child Protective Services to come barging through my door.

Folks were beginning to think my children didn't drink enough milk. I told them we were buying a cow.

Having kiddos with all these broken bones really got to me. I started to worry what people thought about me. I never used to. I never used to care what people said or thought. You either liked me or you didn't. That was up to you, not me. But my children were doing such a bang-up job at looking banged up that I got concerned.

Then there was the whole flashback to newborn sleepless nights. Broken bones hurt. This was something none of my children bargained for. Before they had actually broken anything, they simply wanted the cast or crutches. In all of their childhood wisdom, they failed to comprehend that to receive the apparatus that corrects broken bones, you had to first break a bone. Their little minds and bodies were fairly preoccupied during the day, but at night, when they got still and were trying to sleep, those bones ached and hurt.

Enter Mom stage right.

As moms (and dads), we are tasked with quelling fears and chasing monsters. That is what we do.

We ease pain and heal boo-boos with a kiss. Sometimes in cases like this, our kisses don't work. I'm not one to let any of my children suffer, but if I can avoid pulling out the big guns, I will. I prefer some good-old-fashioned Motrin to some next-level-black-market-street-value painkillers any day of the week. But if my kiddo is in pain, watch out!

Our pediatrician and our orthopedic called in some pretty heavy-duty pain meds for a couple of the kids with some of their more fabulous breaks. A word to the wise: Be careful how you use those. Some of our little ones can't tell us exactly what they're feeling. It will take all your Mom Radar skills to know which medications to dole out and when.

I spent many nights sleeping with or near kiddos with bad breaks. Elliott was one of them. When he broke his arm at school, he snapped that bone in half like a pencil. I know that hurt. Neither of us slept for the first ten days after he broke it. I lived on Starbucks and Excedrin.

After Elliott broke his leg, I hoped we would be finished with the orthopedic surgeon. By this point, we had financed the doctor's last family vacation. But as the old saying goes, "You can hope in one hand, and sh*t in the other. See which one fills up faster!"

In short, we weren't finished. Not by a long shot, although as memory serves, we took about a year off. I think the nursing staff at our orthopedics' office began to miss us.

Elliott isn't really what you would call an athletic type of kid. He is more of my indoor kiddo. So when he came home from school one day and told me was going to try out for the school basketball team, I was surprised. I thought it would be good for him. He seemed pleased with his decision. He was excited about playing basketball at recess with the hopes of getting ready for the tryouts that would happen within the week. The next day—the *very* next day—the school nurse called me.

He. Broke. His. Stinking. Thumb. At. Recess.

I am not even kidding. I have pictures and doctor's notes. Elliott was upset that this little episode cost him the basketball season. I felt bad for him.

Nine months later, we were back in the orthopedics' office with Emma. She stepped off the curb at school and broke her ankle. She was thrilled. She finally got crutches! She was so happy— until she found out how uncomfortable crutches were. Then she wasn't happy at all. We had to live with her for six weeks while she recovered. I seriously thought about having my Xanax prescription refilled.

Sibling rivalry is fun. Brothers and sisters try to get on one another's nerves. It's simply part of growing up. Ethan has been moderately quiet in this chapter—well, aside from getting his head split wide open. Evidently he's made of stronger stuff than the other two. Jeff and I had hoped Ethan, as the oldest, was wiser, the operative word being "hoped."

We were wrong.

One lazy summer afternoon, the kids were roughhousing and Ethan trained his sights on his sister. He claimed he was only moving in to "hug" her. My Mom Radar was screaming, *Um, no dice, kid. Try again.* But I gave him the benefit of the doubt—until Emma could no longer use her right arm.

From what I could tell, during their brother and sister "cuddle time," Emma's right elbow ended up in a compromising position. This not only sent us back to our favorite orthopedic doc, but also landed me in some fairly hot water. Up to this point, most of the kids' injuries occurred on someone else's watch. This was the third injury at *home.*

The kids were asked questions about how, exactly, this happened. Where were your parents when the "accident" happened? Are you afraid at your house? Do you feel safe? Yada yada yada. Our family pediatrician also received a phone call. I'm amazed it took them that long to do some checking. Our pediatrician totally (and truthfully) backed up everything I and the kids had told Dr. Orthopedic. No, my children were not abused. No, these kids were not threatened. Yes, they really were this clumsy.

Thankfully, Emma's elbow wasn't broken, only badly sprained. We left the office in a hot pink full-arm cast three weeks before our annual trip to Port Aransas Beach with my parents. She was scheduled to have the cast removed two days after we returned. No problem. I married MacGyver, and my dad is just as bad as my husband. The two of them relieved Emma of her cast using an array of needle-nose pliers and kitchen knives. Most of the cast simply unraveled. Emma thought it was awesome.

I was horrified. If her elbow had been broken, I would never have agreed to it. But seeing as how this was only a sprain, I allowed Dr. MacGyver and Dr. Frankenstein to proceed so Emma could enjoy the weekend with her grandparents and her brothers.

After the pink cast episode, we didn't have any major catastrophes for a while. None of the children was bucking to be on the next episode of *Ripley's Believe It or Not.* We were doing pretty well—until Jeff took the kids on a trip without me. Now, in all fairness, everything that happened most likely would have happened even if I had been there. Most likely . . .

When the kids were older (eleven, twelve, and thirteen), Jeff took them snow skiing for spring break. I couldn't go. I had gone back to college, and my spring break didn't line up with my children's. It was my last semester before graduation, and one professor told me matter-of-factly that if I chose to miss a week of his class, he would see to it I wouldn't walk across the stage with my peers eight weeks later. What a doll.

So while Jeff and the kids were gone, my sweet hubster would periodically send me proof-of-life pictures of the children enjoying their time sliding, boarding, and tumbling down the Rockies of Colorado. I know that in his heart of hearts, he was making memories of his week as a single dad while desperately trying to keep them all alive. This feeling might have been buried very, very deep by the end of the week.

Monday was the kids' first official full day on the slopes sans ski school or instructors. They were pumped! My husband spent a lot of time on the mountains of Colorado as a kid, and apparently snow skiing is akin to biking riding: a skill that you never truly forget. The one thing he did forget is the fact that none of our three children had ever seen snow, let alone been strapped to a board and sent catapulting down the side of nature's death trap at breakneck speeds. Slight oversight.

Throughout the course of a fun-filled afternoon, he managed to lose *all three kids*. This wasn't simply a "gee I can't see them all right now" thing. No. This was a series of frantic phone calls to the other people on the trip pleading for signs of any of the Louis kids, closely followed by "Please don't mention this to my wife." I can't make this stuff up.

Thank God, while he was on the phone with our dear friend Lesli, our youngest bumbled his way down the slopes, tripping and skidding his way to a stop right in front of her. She told my hubby that she did in fact have two out of three of our kids. That left just one.

The ski patrol took off from the first-aid station at the base of the slopes in the general direction of Ethan's last-known location. Terrific. Lesli kept watch over the two younger ones, and Jeff began to hyperventilate. Ethan had completely wiped out after catching an "edge" left by another snowboarder and was lying in the snow waiting (patiently) for someone to come and rescue him. He wasn't badly hurt—more scared than anything.

This was Ethan's second wipeout for the day. The first rendered his left arm fairly useless, so naturally as he was flying upside down through the air for his next spectacular landing feat, he knew he couldn't land on an already taxed left arm. So he twisted in midair to strategically land on his right arm, effectively injuring it worse than the left. He wagered that rather than get up and try to limp his way down the side of the mountain, he would just lie there in the snow and wait for a daring rescue—effectively scaring the life out of his father in the process. Bonus.

Jeff found Ethan in the first-aid station wearing a new wrist brace and a sling, but otherwise unharmed. But then Jeff needed medical attention for the slight heart attack he experienced.

Do you remember the Spinning Teacup ride? That's where I felt I spent that spring break with all the stories and pictures rolling in from their time at Copper Mountain. The gravity of these events wouldn't fully register until a while after my family arrived back at home—two and a half weeks, to be precise.

It was then that I discovered a small knot under Elliott's right arm. On the outside, I was like "Hmm, how long have you had this? Does it hurt? Let's just go get that looked at. It's no big deal." On the inside, I was screaming, *This is a huge deal! Big! Monster deal!*

Meanwhile, Ethan was still complaining of wrist pain. As I navigated through Houston traffic during morning rush hour to get Elliott to the pediatrician, my snowboarding daredevil rode shotgun. My plan was to kill two birds with one stone and sneak

Evel Knievel into the orthopedic while I was already in the same vicinity visiting the pediatrician.

Well, as the saying goes, the best-laid plans of mice and men often go astray. It appeared that Ethan wasn't the only kid injured over spring break. The family orthopedic couldn't "squeeze" him in for almost a week. Seriously? By this point, he had already been dealing with this irritating type of pain for two and half weeks. We couldn't wait another week.

As we sat in the pediatrician's office waiting for blood work to confirm the doctor's suspicions that Elliott's knot was nothing more than an infected lymph node, she pulled some strings, played her I'm-calling-in-a-professional-favor card, and snagged us an appointment that afternoon with a new orthopedic. Ethan was still wearing the awesomely fabulous ghetto wrist brace that he had acquired from the ski patrol when the doctor walked in with a smile and said, "You're one tough kid. You broke both arms!"

That's when I lost my mind.

Have you ever felt the air being sucked from your lungs while your stomach takes up a new residency somewhere closer to your knees? Yeah. That's about where I found myself. I started to hyperventilate. I couldn't breathe. I couldn't say anything except, "Oh my gosh, Ethan. I am sooooo sorry."

This was my mantra over and over and over again. I might have also thrown in "I'm going to kill your father" a few times. My memories of those first couple of minutes are a bit hazy. Ethan was laughing. The doctor was talking. I was a hundred percent hysterical. I can't think of a time when I completely lost my composure the way I did in that office. Trust me when I tell you that I have turned in some pretty spectacular offerings in this department.

The doctor had to stop dealing with my broken son and come attend to me. He offered me water, tissues, words of comfort, anything he could think of to calm me down. Well, anything except a handful of Xanax. That probably would have been the only thing capable of doing the trick. He even had to send in one of his nurses to remove me from the room and take me to the bathroom to help me get my act together. Not one of my better moments.

When I came back into the room, Ethan was all smiles. He came over to hug me and comfort me and tell me it was "no big deal." No big deal? I'm sorry, but two broken arms is kind of a big deal. I must say that the staff at this doctor's office was exceedingly kind and completely nonjudgmental. Everyone offered me reassurances that this sort of thing happened all the time. Ugh. Kids are resilient and strong.

All in all, no permanent damage was done despite the fact that I made Ethan play baseball during the previous week. Fortunately, he's smart enough to know that he couldn't swing a bat or field the ball. He was the pinch runner. He still managed to slide, arms first, into both first and third bases—twice—with two broken arms. Good grief.

Hubby was perplexed at this diagnosis. The ski patrol had assured him that Ethan's arms weren't broken, because after all, he could move both hands. Here is the deal with the ski patrol: I'm grateful for them. They pulled both my boys off two different mountains and attended to them in their time of need.

Yes, on another day during that eventful spring break, Elliott required an entire *team*—he had to be back-boarded, neck-braced, and given oxygen. (He turned out to be fine—just rattled. Like his sister, he thought some of the things you see on TV aren't as hard as they appear to be. He learned a valuable lesson: Snowboarding is hard.)

But as good as the ski patrol is as first responders, they don't possess X-ray vision. Just because Ethan had nearly complete range of motion in both wrists, virtually no swelling, and zero bruising, that didn't mean his arms were okay. The bottom line is this: Listen to your kids. They typically know when something isn't right with their bodies.

Sometimes you need a little Motrin to ease the swelling; other times, you need a little Xany to help take the edge off. Hey, I'm not judging. Parenting isn't for the faint-hearted!

9.

The Bark Park

When I ran away to California several years ago, I was at the mercy of my sisters. I had no vehicle of my own, so I tagged along wherever they went. One of my sisters wanted to take her dog to the dog park located in Balboa Park. I had never been to a dog park. I thought it might be fun, and besides, I had no other options. Flower, her little Boston terrier, loved to ride in the car. She wasn't much different than a child. In fact, I had no idea just how closely dogs were related to children until that day.

The idea behind a place like the Bark Park is to have a confined area in the city where your dog can run around unleashed and be free. They can play with other dogs and bark and have a good time. I was amazed at all the different types of dogs. Little bitty Chihuahuas, midsize mutts, and even some very large, strap-a-saddle-on-them Great Danes. Everyone was playing, and everyone was getting along. The owners were standing in little groups watching their "kids" play. You could hear the conversations between the dogs as they went racing by:

Flower: Chase me!

Other dog: No, you chase me!

Next dog: Run this way!

Flower: Okay!

Then off they would zoom, back and forth and back and forth. I found myself getting as nervous for Flower as I would for my own kids had we been at a people park. But Flower, like my kids, was making her own way. She was having fun. She was on a level playing field with all the dogs—until someone pulled out the *toy*.

With the arrival of that one toy, the earth's rotation shifted. Groups of dogs that had been running and playing in perfect peace now turned on one another, baring their teeth and growling. Flower started chasing a dog and then jumped on the dog's owner when he bent down to pick up his own dog. My poor sister had to run all the way across the park to catch her. Flower didn't want to listen to my sister. She didn't want to leave the park. In fact, it was a bizarre battle of wills to see who would actually win.

Everything went upside down because of a Frisbee.

This is exactly how it is with children. Odd power struggles occur every day. Our kids will constantly test their boundaries. We know that no matter where we set the limits, they will push and push until they get one toe over the line and then stand there to see what we're going to do about it. The only comfort is in knowing that they do this with their friends too. So they aren't just testing their parents—they're testing everyone in their world.

When my kids were in preschool, very seldom did they come home without a note informing me that one of them had bitten someone. At the preschool my kids attended, the teachers would write these very sweet "happy face" notes at the end of the day. I looked forward to those notes. I cherished these notes. But they weren't as frequent a visitor in our house as their counterpart, the "sad face" note.

What you didn't want to see in your child's cubby was a red note—the "sad face" note—informing you that Junior had had a lot of difficulties that day. Not one redeeming quality could be found to give him a "happy face" note. Because I had three kids in the same preschool, you could bet dollars to doughnuts that at least one of them every Tuesday or Thursday was going to have a red note in their cubby. It was a super-double-terrific day when there was more than one red note on the same day.

Cry.

As I mentioned, we referred to Elliott as our little piranha. What I failed to divulge is that the other two fit that category as well. All three of them were champion biters. They came by it honestly. My mother was notorious for her biting. I am pretty sure she bit her friends until she was ten or eleven. Stories about my mother and her biting are epic in parts of the Texas Hill Country. So I'm going with genetics on this one.

My theory behind the biting is two-fold. One, it's about a good old-fashioned power struggle. Someone has a toy that someone else wants. When they don't get their way, they bare their teeth—literally.

Two, when you're as little in size as my kids were and a bigger kid starts pushing you around, your chompers become the most effective means of self-defense. The threat can be real or perceived. Either way, the teeth will be shown and someone is probably going to bleed.

I was convinced that my kids would be the first ever kicked out of this Christian preschool for cannibalism. I simply couldn't get a handle on the biting thing. The kicker was they did it only at school. At least in the beginning. Each one of my children had received so many red notes that I could have repapered the downstairs bathroom—which translated to a lot of teeth marks on their friends.

The school administration is bound by certain limitations. They can carry out only certain types of discipline. All my little savages were read to—sweet little books about how we bite apples and not our friends. Give me a break. When you have a two-year-old purposefully going for blood, reading her a book about biting apples won't get the message across. They also sat in time-out at school. That was probably a safe bet, but all it really did was give them time to plot out their next attack.

I'm a visual learner. I learn best when I can see what I'm supposed to be learning. You can tell me what you want me to learn, but if you *show* me while you tell me, I have a much better chance of retaining that information. Our children operate on the same level. Every time I would get to school and see one of those stinking red notes sticking out of a cubby, I'd first engage the filter over my mouth to keep from spitting fire at my sweet innocents and then wrack my brain to figure out how to tell them so they'd understand that biting their friends would chase them all away.

But again, when you talk to a two- or a three-year-old, reason just doesn't play a very big role. I needed a way to *show* them. As it turns out, I just needed to be patient. One by one, the kids forgot who they were dealing with. They forgot that I am their mother and not one of their little friends from school, so when they came at me with an open mouth, fangs bared—I bit them back.

Again, I have to stress to you, I didn't hurt my children. I would never hurt them. I did get their attention, though. I had my moment. I had the opportunity to *tell* them that biting hurts and *show* them how it hurts. While they left full upper and lower teeth marks in me, I left no such marks on them, but the act of biting them registered high on the "hurt feelings" scale. Up until that point, they had been told several times that biting hurt, but they didn't actually connect the dots until *they were bitten*.

After that, we stopped getting so many red notes from school.

Parenting is all about timing. You have to be patient and be able to outlast your children. They have the advantage in this department, I'm afraid to say, so we must be vigilant. Kids are very smart; they know when you're bluffing. They know when you're running on low-battery life and the threats you're giving don't really hold water.

Take car seats. For some reason, remaining buckled goes against every fiber of their being. They don't understand that we didn't invent car seats to deliver endless hours of torture and punishment to them. They don't understand that if they don't remain securely fastened in their seats, they could get hurt or Mom could get a ticket from the local law and run the risk of losing her strong-willed children to the authorities.

All they know is that this five-point harness system is the devil and imposes an immediate threat to their well-being and mental health. They must fight, fight, fight to the death with everything inside their tiny bodies to rid themselves of these horrible, evil contraptions.

Ethan screamed so much each time we put him in his car seat, you would have thought we installed hot pokers or sharp nails on the back side of his seat. Don't children like riding in cars? That's the way they look on TV. All the children in the movies seem to calm right down when Mom or Dad put them in the car. In fact, that was the one way their parents could calm them down when all else had failed.

Not my son.

He screamed until I thought he would choke. I would have to pull over halfway to the grocery store (which was a whopping ten minutes from my house), climb into the back seat, and check to make sure I hadn't done something terribly wrong. To my relief and dismay, the straps were fine. From all the racket he was making, you'd think—or at least hope—there would be a reason. No, he was simply mad. This went on and on and on until he was old enough to face forward.

Amanda, a sweet friend of mine, went through something similar with her daughter. The difference is that her daughter was four years old. This kid is super smart and knew exactly how to push Mom's buttons. As the two of them were leaving my house one late afternoon, goodbyes were especially hard, and her daughter was having a difficult time getting out the front door. I offered to "help." I carried all their stuff (the bag, shoes, miscellaneous clothing) to the car while Amanda struggled to get a good grip on her wiggling, screaming child.

"I don't wanna go home! I wanna stay for dinner! I just wanna eat dinner here! Don't take me!"

Amanda managed to get this pint-sized prizefighter into the back seat and into her car seat but didn't get her buckled yet. This peanut didn't weigh very much, so a five-point harness system was still required for her safety. Amanda had succeeded in fastening one side of the leg straps when all of a sudden, in a move of sheer genius on her daughter's part, she screamed, "You're hurting me!"

Amanda's hands flew into the air, and she raised up and backed away so fast from her child that she hit her head on the top of her car. The best part of the whole thing was the smug, satisfied look on her four-year-old's face. She had just struck pure baby-guilt gold. Amanda turned around and looked at me. She stood slowly, leaving her enraged daughter to sit and scream in the car, and with tears in her own eyes, she asked, "What do I do?"

Folks, I am here to tell you, buckle them in. Amanda was in no way, shape, or form hurting her daughter. She was doing the right thing by obeying the law and keeping her child safe by keeping her in a car seat. Had her child been allowed to roam freely through the car, she would have endangered her life as well as her mother's by climbing from the back to the front and back again with Amanda trying to referee.

I put my hands on Amanda's shoulders, looked her square in

the eye, and told her to finish what she had started. "Buckle her in. Use your big-girl voice (not your yelling voice—there's a difference) and remind her that you're the parent, and you will win this round."

I have said before that certain battles are not necessarily hills to die on (remember the hair conditioner in the bathtub?), but this particular one is. Your child's safety is a life-and-death issue. Buckle them in.

I climbed into the driver's seat to watch how this was all going to end and was pleased to see that Amanda did get her daughter securely buckled. But she was still screaming her sweet little head clean off and Amanda was suffering greatly from mommy guilt, so she came at her little one with a peace offering in the form of an iPod touch. She quickly batted it away in anger. Amanda reached for it again to try one more time, but I picked it up instead. You can't reward abominable behavior with something fun.

Stand your ground. Be the parent. So what if they cry all the way home? Let them. How do you deal with noise on that level every time you get into the vehicle? A really loud radio. It will take only two or three times of you outlasting them on issues like these for them to realize who's actually in control.

Mealtimes are also a fun household battleground. We've gone many rounds over "What's for dinner?" in our kitchen. The most popular answer from me is "Whatever I put in front of you."

Pureed peas are just about the most disgusting and unappealing food you can purchase in the grocery store. They look funny and they smell worse. But they're essential for your baby's proper growth. In fact, if you stand in the baby food aisle of your local supermarket and take a good look at all the jarred choices, you'll find just about every vegetable and fruit or combination of the two known to man. It's really important that our children have a balanced diet and start off with the proper foundation.

Peas are probably my least favorite food in the whole wide world—and I will try almost anything. I have vivid memories of my mother serving peas with dinner and me shoveling spoonfuls of them into my mouth and swallowing them whole with my milk to keep from having to chew or taste them. Even so, peas are a staple in my home. I still don't like them, but I fix them for my children. I have fed them peas since they were babies sitting in their high chairs. I want them to be healthy. (Plus, as you remember, frozen peas make excellent ice packs.)

I have two pretty decent eaters and one challenge. Guess who the picky one is.

Before I had children, I would often say some version of "I'll never [fill in the blank]": "I'll never supplement a bottle for the breast." "I'll never use the TV as a sitter." "I'll never feed my child a cereal bottle." My all-time top pre-child saying was "My child will never act like that."

Emma was a difficult baby to feed. She quit nursing very early, most likely because I was already pregnant with her brother (extra helping of mommy guilt on that one), so the bottle became her best friend. Sleep deprivation makes you entertain all sorts of ideas—like putting rice cereal into your six-week-old's bottle. My mother-in-law first tried to spoon-feed it to her. No dice. Then we thought that putting cereal in her nighttime bottle might be more effective. It was liquid gold. She was in hog heaven. She sucked it right down—every last drop. Then she slept for six hours straight. Of course, that first night, I was up every thirty minutes checking on her, making sure she was still breathing!

As she got older, it became more and more of a challenge to find things to put in front of my up-and-coming food critic.

Once Emma learned how to talk, her most favorite thing to say was "Is this old?" I have no idea where she got this. I would hand her a sippy cup of milk, fresh from the fridge, and she would take it and look from me to the cup and back to me again and, with the voice of an angel, ask, "Momma, is this old?" It blew my mind.

Plates of food freshly spooned out of the pans on the stove would get the same quizzical looks, followed by the same question. This went on for two and a half *years*. People thought we had expiration-date issues at my house. Emma doesn't remember that phase, but she still subjects all food, both perishables and nonperishables, to almost daily expiration-date checks.

Another big issue with her was the whole meat thing. Every meat I served in my house was chicken. It didn't matter if it was actually chicken or not. In her mind, and for the sanity of the other members of the family, we ate chicken every night. Allow me to explain.

Emma really liked chicken. She still does. She thought she didn't like other meats, but she ate pot roast, steak, pork chops, and even various sausages. Here's the deal: When she was much younger, we (I can't remember who started this) got into the habit of telling her to eat her chicken. It stuck. She is now firmly past this stage but still thinks the only meat I know how to cook is chicken. For some of my friends, this wouldn't be such a bad thing—only serving chicken, that is.

I know plenty of moms out there who behave every night as though they were short-order cooks. You know the types—the ones who make a kid-friendly meal consisting of chicken nuggets or hotdogs with mac and cheese on the side. Then they make a completely different grown-up meal for themselves and their spouse. For those of you who operate your homes this way, can I ask you why you go through the trouble to make two separate meals? Isn't it exhausting?

I get the fact that chicken nuggets with a helping of mac and cheese isn't exactly what most adults would like to have for dinner. I mean, I wouldn't eat that for dinner. Do you know that the kids will eat what you put in front of them? I promise, they will. Maybe not at first, but Junior will get hungry enough to eat what's put on his plate.

My dad is a chef. Well, he used to be before he started with the whole big-rig trucking thing. In my opinion, he's one of the best chefs in the country. I grew up eating some fairly bizarre things because Daddy wanted to expand my palate. He wanted to expose my sisters and me to all sorts of various foods and flavors. For instance, while most folks across the country celebrated Thanksgiving dinner with a traditional corn bread dressing, we had an oyster-based dressing.

One of Daddy's favorite kitchen pantry staples was dried seaweed—he liked making his own sushi rolls. Another favorite dish that frequented our refrigerator was a Korean fermented-vegetable recipe known as kimchi. He wanted us to eat our veggies so we would grow up to be big and strong. He also wanted to be able to take his four children anywhere and feed us from the menu or (this is super important) take us to anyone's house without embarrassment.

If all we had been exposed to were chicken nuggets, hotdogs, and macaroni and cheese, what in the world would we eat at Mark and Stephanie's house for dinner, who, incidentally, did not have any children and decided to serve roasted duck? Can you imagine the horror or the embarrassment my parents—or any parent— would suffer if a plate of food set before their child at a friend's house was greeted with "That looks disgusting. I'm not eating it"?

My dad also knew that one day we would grow up, leave home, and have homes of our own. The skills we picked up from him are invaluable. Don't get me wrong, I make a mean chicken nugget, but my boeuf bourguignon is even better. I realize that not everyone has had the opportunity to learn from someone like my dad, but to borrow a phrase from *Ratatouille*, "Anyone can cook."

If you can read, you can cook. I do believe Betty Crocker still has a cookbook out there. There's also a little thing called the internet. Several food websites—Food.com, Kraftfoods.com, and Allrecipes.com are just a few—will take the ingredients you have on hand and help you plan a family-friendly meal in minutes. You can even reach out to me, and I'll help you through your kitchen struggles.

Think about this: If the only things our kids eat are chicken nuggets, hotdogs, or mac and cheese with the occasional fruit cup thrown in there, where is the balance of nutrition? We all learned about the food pyramid in health class in elementary school. There are four basic food groups, and although I just mentioned four different foods, I didn't cover all four food groups.

I have a friend whose seven-year-old son survives on chicken nuggets and Tater Tots. But they have to be certain chicken nuggets—no off-brand—and the Tater Tots have to be Ore-Ida. She swears that if she even tries to put anything else on his plate and in front of him, he gags. The last well-balanced meal he had was when he was still in the high chair. So what does she do? She makes two dinners every night: one for him and one for herself and her husband.

Okay, so maybe that isn't such a big deal (I really do think it's a big deal, but for argument's sake, let's say for right now that it isn't). If you have only one child, logistically you could microwave something quickly. What if you have six children? No joke, I have another friend who has six children. I asked her how she cooked dinner. She was confused by my question. I rephrased it: "Do you cook one thing for dinner or do you let each child decide what they would like to have each night?"

It took her a full ten minutes to stop laughing. When she caught her breath, she said, "Are you crazy? It would take *all day* just for one meal if I let each of them choose what they wanted for dinner! No. I decide. They can either eat it or not. That's their choice."

Finally! Someone with some sense.

For the record, let me iterate that although I do cook on average five nights a week, my children don't always greet my culinary experiments with an open mind and a willing stomach. At times, I am greeted with "Uh, Mom? What exactly is this?"

Yes, there have been nights when dinner didn't turn out the way it was supposed to and the pizza delivery guy had to be called in to save the day. But the bottom line is that I tried and they attempted to eat it.

In all seriousness, what do you do when Junior refuses to eat? At our house, we kissed her (it was usually Emma) good night and put her to bed. She wasn't going to starve. Breakfast was served at six forty-five in the morning.

I would tell the kid who refused to eat, "If I go to the trouble of cooking something, you better believe you'll put out the effort to eat it. I'm not going to poison you. The food in front of you won't kill you. This isn't a new perk I discovered in the *1001 Ways to Slowly Torture Your Kids Handbook*. It's dinner. It covers the four basic food groups. It's good for you. Do us both a favor and eat it. If that's too much to ask, sweet dreams. I love you and we'll see you in the morning."

I know that may be more than some of you can handle. If you don't trust me, ask your pediatrician. He or she will tell you the same thing. Your kids won't starve. Eventually, they will eat.

This is hard work. You must be consistent. If you waiver on this today and try to stand firm tomorrow, they will remember. And then they will push and push and push until they wear you down. Are you ready for that? Today the struggle is over green

peas and roast beef, but tomorrow, it will be over a ten-thirty curfew versus a midnight curfew or dating one on-one versus groups
of people. Stand your ground. Be the parent.

Finally, let me just ask you: Aren't you tired? If you work
outside the home, once you have fought the traffic, picked up the
kids, and walked through the door, do you really want to make
more than one dinner? Do you even want to make just *one* dinner?
Hold everything if it happens to be baseball, soccer, or football
season. Those weeknight practices will eat you alive. For those of
us with girls—well, we have dance, gymnastics, and, my personal
favorite, art lessons twice a week. My head is beginning to throb
just thinking about all of that.

Realistically, if you're blessed to get off work by four o'clock,
you could have your kids picked up by four-thirty. Then you're
getting home by five o'clock, long enough to change clothes and
hustle off to the ball field. Where's dinner? Drive-through? Homework is done in the vehicle.

Would you like to know a secret? Ten-pound packages of
hamburger meat. That is one of my secrets to hectic seasons of
ball games and practices. I buy ten-pound packages of hamburger
meat, brown it, bag it, in one-and-a-half-pound bags, and freeze
it. Voilà! Dinner is halfway made. Hamburger Helper is my BFF
during game seasons! They can eat it in the truck from a plastic cup with a disposable spoon on the way to the ball field. It's
cheaper than a drive-through. Throw some frozen peas into the
pan while the noodles are cooking and you have a full meal in
one pan. Frozen peas are my answer to a lot of things. Funny how
I don't like to eat them, though.

On non-season nights, the schedule is basically the same. You
still have to pick up the kids. They will still have homework. At
some point during the week, they'll need to bathe. That's always a
fun sport in my house: chasing the boys down. They don't seem to

understand that they need to shower more than once every three days. It must be the Y-chromosome.

The rest of the house still needs attention. Laundry will forever need to be done. I know in my house we must have gremlins. It's utterly exhausting keeping up with the laundry. It never ends. Then on top of all those things, we still (many of us) have a spouse. It's during that special quiet time of the night—the kids are in bed, the dog is asleep by the couch, the TV volume has been reduced to a dull roar, and you are standing alone at the kitchen sink. You're finishing up the last of the dinner dishes, when who walks up behind you and lays a gentle hand on your shoulder? Yep. Mr. Frisky. You know with one touch, one little touch, what that means.

But you have just spent the last four hours in the kitchen making each one of your kids a different meal. You are bone-tired. In this corner of the Bark Park, the kids reign supreme. They have won, and they don't even realize how great their victory is, but I would wager you and your spouse are feeling how great your loss is becoming.

Power struggles come in all shapes and sizes. We have them over the food we serve our family. We have them over the inbred need to defend our property and ourselves, whether that threat is real or perceived. Power struggles pop up between a husband and a wife when it comes to the way they will discipline and handle their children. All of these are just part of the Bark Park of life.

So which pack will you run with?

10.

Anger Management

Picture this: A rocking chair, a sleeping infant, a smiling and peaceful mommy quietly humming a beautiful lullaby as she rocks her chubby baby girl to dreamland. Now fast-forward two years. That baby girl is still precious, though no longer chubby, and still has her beautiful blue eyes closed, only this time they are pinched tight while her mouth is stretched as wide open as it will go. The sound vibrating off the walls of your home is nothing like the lullaby that once echoed serenely. Now it is an ear-piercing shriek coming from an angry two-year-old learning the intricacies of every parent's nightmare: The Temper Tantrum.

Those spectacular displays of energy will test parents to their absolute breaking point. How do I know? I have been there—and back.

Every child is different. Every tantrum is different. But every child possesses the skills to send Mom or Dad or both diving for the safety of their closets at any given moment. The best part of this twisted new reality? We never outgrow The Tantrum. We only get better at properly throwing one.

I've spent the better part of the book so far airing my children's dirty laundry. Would you like a sneak peek into some of mine? I thought you might. I come from a long line of champion fit-throwers. Champion German fit-throwers. Champion German, Southern fit-throwers. I personally possess a unique set of skills that make most Oscar-winning performances look like child's play.

Having said that, I don't often bring those skills to the table. Through the years, I've learned the importance of anger management. But once in a while, even the most mild-mannered and self-controlled princess loses her head. Certain people I'm forced to deal with (ahem, family—why is it always family?) really push my buttons. I can't explain the visceral reaction I have when I'm around them. What I can tell you is that Suzie Homemaker leaves the building and is promptly replaced with the Wicked Witch of the East: curses fly, walls crumble, and shear devastation rains down.

Try this on for size: We were having a little get-together at our house one summer. Charley-Girl, our (I say "our," but I really mean "my") golden retriever puppy was thirteen months old. I was incredibly attached to that dog. Honestly, my attachment bordered on obsession.

Contrary to popular belief, puppies don't necessarily like to swim. They instinctively know how to swim, but wanting to swim isn't an automatic given. I had been working with Charley-Girl to ease her into our pool so she could get used to the water. I didn't want to scare her or drown her.

Well, apparently my visiting in-laws figured they knew much better than I about how to teach my dog to swim. Before I knew what was happening, my precious Charley-Girl was five feet in the air above the pool. Someone had picked her up and thrown her into the air, and she landed on her back—she landed upside down!—in the middle of the water. You may think that isn't a major problem. After all, she's a dog. True, but she was a baby, a baby deathly afraid of the water, and she had just been thrown into the water.

I completely lost it.

I jumped into the pool where Charley was frantically clawing at the water trying to get out. She was snorting and coughing up water. I was so mad I had steam coming off me. All conversation on my patio ceased immediately. My husband took a tentative step toward me as he tried to shield his family for what he knew was coming. It didn't work. I exploded. "Are you crazy? Why in the world would you do such a stupid thing? She can't swim! Are trying to kill my dog?"

Bear in mind that I had a backyard full of people. And still I continued to scream the same words over and over. My rant ended with something along the lines of "This party is over!" I pointed a finger at the offender. "You can get out!" Everyone was all too happy to vacate the premises of such a crazy lady. I can't remember if they've been back. Maybe once or twice. I locked Charley in my bedroom. No one was allowed to see her.

Temper tantrums will jump up and bite you when you least expect them. I'm a grown woman. I had no idea I still had that type of fight in me. Some folks just bring out the worst in us. Unfortunately, our precious baby children will try to evoke some of those same feelings. The only difference is they seriously can't help it. When a two-year-old is having a nuclear core meltdown in the middle of aisle thirteen at the local grocery store, she isn't trying to drive you crazy. She simply doesn't know any other way to express herself.

Communication is a huge deal for our little peanuts. They learn new words, new motions—new everything—that fill up their world at an incredible rate. They learn a multitude of new sights and sounds every day. So when Junior is flipping out in the local Food Mart, chances are his mind is in overdrive about something. The question is, What do you do? Do you react? Or do you respond?

When Emma was eighteen months old, she was diagnosed with

sensory integration disorder (SID). Have you ever heard of that? It was new to me. In fact, I told my pediatrician that she didn't need to make up fake disorders to make me feel better about my abysmal parenting skills. Her diagnosis came off the cuff as she witnessed Emma completely losing her cool when the TV in the exam room turned to "snow" after the movie ended. She asked me a series of odd questions about Emma:

Doc: Does she stay dressed?

Me: No. She hates clothes.

Doc: Will she eat yogurt? Or mashed potatoes?

Me: Yes, to yogurt. No, to mashed potatoes, but she will eat a baked potato.

Doc: When you hand her a toy or a cup, will she cross her midpoint or will she take the object with whichever hand is closer?

Me: The closer hand.

She gave me the name and number of a behavior specialist to have Emma tested. The specialist confirmed she had SID. Basically, her brain was wired differently. It was almost as though the two halves of her brain were on strike against each other and didn't want to communicate. As a result, Emma was extremely sensitive to everything in her environment Her clothes overwhelmed her, so she took them off. The hem inside her socks drove her crazy, so she didn't wear socks or shoes—for years.

As frustrating as this was for me, it was doubled for Emma. For a couple of years, all she did was cry. Her outbursts of rage would stop my heart.

Do you remember the neighbors of ours who don't have any children? They liked to hang out in my backyard. Fortunately, they also provided some much-needed intervention on occasion. When Emma was two and started turning out some spectacular screaming fits, Elliott was one and Ethan was three. One crying child is often enough to get the others going. More times than a few, I found myself with a fussing Elliott on my hip, walking next door for some help.

Mr. Mike would take Elliott from me, and I'd walk back into the war zone that was my house: Emma would be screaming in the time-out spot and Ethan would be pouting on the couch. I would pace in their foyer for about ten minutes until I caught my breath.

Sometimes Mommy needed a time-out.

Praise the Lord Emma outgrew those years! But she wasn't the only one to provide fodder for this chapter. Elliott has had some special moments of his own. I can't say exactly where he picked up his unique set of skills. Perhaps they're genetic. I'd hate to think that my side of the family plagued my sweet baby with his temperament, but the jury is certainly leaning in that direction.

As I mentioned previously, Elliott was my champion biter, like my mother. He stopped biting people, but over the years, he took his anger out on objects. When he was twelve or so, I was upstairs one morning attempting to vacuum the black hole that was his room. As parents, we spend a great deal of our time cleaning up after our offspring. They seem to have Mess-Making 101 hard-wired into their little brains.

That day, I noticed an odd array of wood chips scattered across the floor. Hmm. While my husband is quite handy around the house, we currently didn't have any home improvement projects going. Even if he were to bust out the jigsaw, hacksaw, or any other type of woodworking tool, they're restricted to the confines of the garage, not my son's upstairs bedroom. I began to investigate.

After I picked up enough stray pieces of notebook paper to make the western half of the forested United States cry, spare parts to the latest machine he was taking apart, and all the dirty clothes he had worn for the last two weeks, I still hadn't found the source of the wood chips. Nothing on his floor suggested a woodworking project. Judging by all the machine parts, he was quite possibly trying to build a robot. But to my knowledge, he wasn't carving one out of wood. Having cleared the floor of the major debris, I continued with my vacuuming endeavor.

I should probably inform y'all that Elliott spends a great deal of time in his room. Both as his choice and as a form of punishment. He likes his room. It's filled with things he enjoys. When the choice to go to his room is his, he is one happy kid. But when he's sent to his room, suddenly the walls morph into a dungeon, chains drop from the ceiling, and spikes spring up from the floor. At least that's the best I can guess. He hates being sent to his room. I can't for the life of me understand why there is such a huge difference between those two occasions other than his free will has been removed.

Once I finished vacuuming, I remembered that his sheets needed to be changed. As I pulled back his comforter and top sheet, I saw it. On the edge of his bed was a three-and-a-half-inch gash. I dropped to my knees to get a better look. Elliott's bed is made of pine. Sure as I live and breathe, a chunk had been carved out of the sideboard. I sat there trying to comprehend what in the world I was looking at—and how he could have pulled this off. I would have to wait until he got home from school for my answer.

As luck would have it, Elliott was in no mood to play nice with anyone in the house that afternoon. So I sent him off to his room to prevent him from "hulking out" on the rest of the family. After about ten minutes, I crept upstairs to see what he did while he was suffering in exile. I opened his door and found him lying across his bed, arms touching the floor, his head hanging down over the side—wait for it—gnawing on the side of his bed. Are you kidding me! I seriously thought we had termites! Turns out I've been raising a woodchuck!

. . .

While Emma gave me a run for my money as a baby, Ethan and Elliott saved their antics for late elementary school. Ethan liked to run away from home. We have rules at our house, and sometimes those rules put a real damper on our kids' social agenda. The funny thing about his "running away," he always came home when either he got hungry or it got dark.

Ethan is a really smart kid. In fact, he's so smart that school began to bore him in about the fifth grade. Homework began to get under his skin. He couldn't understand why he had to do his homework when he could go in and ace the test. Busy work drove him nuts. At his school, an incomplete assignment or a late assignment earned the student a Responsibility Form. I, the parent, had to sign the form, as did the student and the teacher. In theory, the student should receive only three of these forms per semester—anything beyond that resulted in detention. Ethan received *thirty-nine* his second semester of fifth grade. I was beside myself.

Here's the kicker: He still made the honor roll at the end of the year.

During our continual struggles with the homework battles of fifth grade, Jeff and I needed to get creative with how we got Ethan's attention. As a pre-pubescent, he was dealing with enough hormones to wage a chemical war on a small foreign country. Yet this was an unknown concept to him. According to him, we were the enemy, and therefore, he would strike at us in any way he could. One of his favorite pastimes was slamming his bedroom door. He was exceptionally good at this—so good, in fact, that when he slammed his door upstairs, my pictures would rattle on the walls downstairs. I warned him that was unacceptable behavior.

He informed me that the degree of his concern was less than zero. That was fine. He couldn't care less. I could totally fix that. Jeff was out of town on business, so after I took Ethan to school the next day, I called in a favor from our neighbor. Mike came over and without incident quickly removed Ethan's bedroom door. My neighbors are really wonderful people. If I could have handpicked the best people to live next door to, I couldn't have done any better.

Mike took the door to his house for safekeeping and then came back for the box of goodies I didn't think Ethan would need for the foreseeable future: his X-Box, his TV, and his DVD player. We decided to leave his computer. Mike is a computer genius by trade, and he helped me install a password that only the two of us knew. Leaving the computer in Ethan's room was a slow, deliberate source of torture.

When Ethan got home from school that day, the only usable thing in his room was his bed. I informed him that I wasn't mad, but that he was in desperate need of some anger management. Until he learned how to control his temper and become a calm and quiet member of our household, this was his new reality. He didn't seem too irritated—after all I had left his computer. The dam broke when he tried to turn it on. One month later, he began to get his privileges back. (Yes, it took him a month.)

Evidently his intelligence is limited to the world of academia because Ethan took a really, really long time before he stopped testing the strength and voltage of his electric fence.

He survived his fifth- and sixth-grade years at school, often repeating the same offenses many times. As I mentioned, the kids went to parochial school and I needed to take them to school every day. Getting Ethan into the car at our house on a school day was a magic trick worthy of David Copperfield or Criss Angel. The kid simply didn't want to go. On more than one day, I pulled him from the house and shoved him into the truck still in his pajamas.

He thought that there was no way I would make him attend classes in his PJs. He was mistaken. The school principal stood at the car rider line and greeted every student every morning. He knew their names, their family, and their backstory. He was very familiar with all the stunts my little genius had pulled in recent history. He also knew that my husband traveled for work four to five days a week. So it was no surprise to him that when I pulled up on that morning, two of my kids hopped right out of the truck and one did not. I rolled down the passenger window and told him I needed some assistance.

He climbed into my truck and had a man-to-man chat with my kid in the back seat of my Expedition. To this day, I don't know what words of wisdom Mr. Goldsmith imparted to my son. Frankly, I don't care. All I know is that five minutes after he entered my vehicle, he and my wayward child climbed out. I handed Ethan a bag full of clothes, and he was ready to face his day.

My dear husband's extensive work travel throughout our marriage has occasionally presented an interesting dynamic when it comes to disciplining our more strong-willed child. Make no mistake, I am not one to shy away from setting my children straight. But sometimes my stature doesn't present quite the same intimidation factor as it would if I, too, possessed a Y-chromosome.

Case in point: Ethan's seventh grade was a rough year. I would wager that most seventh-grade boys have difficult years. They are full of hormones, they aren't sure if they are little kids or big kids, and the only thing they know for certain is that they don't want their mothers telling them what to do. Their emotions are always close to the surface, particularly their anger. This is where we found ourselves one Sunday morning.

Jeff had left at the crack of dawn for a two-and-a-half-week business trip to India. India. Do you have any idea how far away India is from Texas? Trust me when I tell you it's very far. Well, apparently Ethan had been studying his geography as well because as soon as Jeff went wheels up, Ethan went horns out and morphed into a miniature monster.

It just so happened that this particular Sunday was his turn to acolyte at church. That's our denomination's version of being the altar boy. He decided to opt out. After struggling and arguing with him for nearly thirty minutes, I gave up. The two younger ones and I left the house without him.

When I arrived at church, I looked for our friends the McCoys and told them about Ethan. David and Lesli seem to always be in the right place at the right time. David, otherwise known as Big Mac, is a virtual mountain of man, standing at six five and weighing 285 pounds. He was irritated with my son for a couple of reasons: First, Ethan was shirking his responsibilities at church. He signed up to acolyte and should be there to do just that. Second, the level of disrespect Ethan showed me was unacceptable. I, as his mother, told him we were leaving. He, as the child, should have replied with "Yes, ma'am" or "Okay." He did neither.

Big Mac looked me square in the face and asked, "How do I get into your house without ringing the doorbell?"

I gawked at him. He was dead serious. He was about to drive over to my house and haul my heathen child to church for me.

I handed Big Mac my house key and wished him good luck. He assured me he didn't need it. The two of them would return shortly in plenty of time for the service. I took my other two to Sunday school and found a quiet place to sit with Lesli.

Our church is close to our house, which is wired with a security camera monitoring system. In short, I can see into every room in the house. Rather than attending our own Sunday school class that morning, Lesli and I watched the latest episode of *Lifestyles of the Young and Defiant*. We saw Big Mac pull into the driveway and let himself into the house. The dogs were very happy to see him. Useless guard dogs.

Big Mac moved up the stairs and across the playroom into Ethan's room completely undetected. What was Ethan doing? Sitting at his desk, headphones on, playing a video game. Big Mac stood right behind him for a solid count of ten to fifteen seconds before he spoke. Although we could see what was going on, we couldn't hear anything. When Big Mac made his presence known, Ethan jumped about three feet in the air.

It was priceless.

Ten minutes later, Ethan was dressed and on his way to fulfill his duties and apologize to his mother. Lesli and I were crying with laughter at the thought of what Big Mac had said to him. Was it mean of me to find so much entertainment in that moment? Perhaps. But here's the deal: Ethan is the child, and I am the parent. Granted, he didn't know how to master his emotions. Anger is a particularly difficult emotion to get a hold of—for anyone. Toddlers throw tantrums. Teenagers slam doors. Adults use words and some even resort to violence—take a look at the news today. Anger is the trickiest of all the emotions to channel.

But it's also necessary.

At times we need anger to spur us on to do better and try harder and to even keep us safe. Anger can transform into passion, if we learn how to properly manage it. We can't let it master us. Think about anger this way: When someone, say another child, wrongs our child, our first response is to meet with that child's parent to defend our child. Immediately our defenses go up to protect, defend, and shelter our child. We're angry. We become passionate.

Yet if we go into that type of situation with our "guns blazing," so to speak, we put the other parent on the defensive as well. Not much will get accomplished. But if we turn that anger into something positive or at least dial it back long enough to get all the facts about the situation at hand, then we stand a fighting chance of getting to the bottom of the original problem. Otherwise, we only add fuel to an already raging fire.

Anger management. It sounds like a great plan in theory, but it's exceptionally difficult to execute. Parenting is brutal—rewarding—but brutal. We must learn to first master our own emotions before we can teach our little ones how to control theirs. Can it be done? Yes. Will we fail miserably on some days? Absolutely. And if you're anything like me, your fails will be legendary.

But despite all of that, don't give up. And don't lose heart! One day, you'll be able to look back on these days with a sigh and a smile and be thankful you lived to tell the tale.

11.

The Shake Weight, Lip Liner, and a Paint Can

When my kids were babies, I retired from church work to devote more time to raising them. As I mentioned, I like to have things all laid out and to know exactly what my next step will be. Well, choosing to stay home full-time was no exception. But life doesn't always turn out the way we plan. As the kids got older, I started working outside the home. Jeff was in between careers, and we needed the extra income.

In April a couple of years later, after Jeff had established a thriving new business, I decided to take a much-needed break. I gave my boss two weeks' notice, eager for some downtime.

I wanted to get back to writing and to working out at the gym. Summer is always right around the corner when you live in Houston. It's never too early to start getting ready for the dreaded swimsuit season. But close to a month after my last day at work, I still hadn't made it to the gym. Not once. I hadn't had one spare hour to myself.

The trouble had begun weeks before when I came home from work to find contractors in my house. I was surprised, although in retrospect, I really shouldn't have been. Jeff had mentioned in passing that he wanted to make a few minor changes to the house—the floors in the upstairs bathrooms, for starters. Both the upstairs bathrooms were half carpet and half tile. I don't know who came up with that brilliant idea. We bought the house already built, and when we moved in, I had a brand-new, two-week-old baby boy. That wasn't the ideal time for a remodel job!

Well, I hadn't been pregnant in a long, long time, so he must have figured it was safe to rip out the old flooring and lay down the new. We had also discussed replacing the carpet upstairs. It was thirteen-year-old, builder-grade carpet that had survived three kids, numerous bottles and sippy cups, and countless contraband snacks, not to mention the hair dye stains contributed by my younger sister while she lived with us. It was time for something new.

On top of that, we talked about how we weren't using the house to its fullest potential. Upstairs, there are four bedrooms, two bathrooms, and one large playroom. (The master bedroom is downstairs.) We were using only two of the bedrooms, one bathroom, and the playroom—that was the only room big enough to house the Lego factory.

My "office" was upstairs toward the back of the house. Jeff thought it was safer to put me in the back of the house because I am what some people call a creative and others a disaster. At one time, the boys were in separate bedrooms, but then my little sister moved in, and we put the boys together in one room. Emma has always had her own room.

We needed to make some adjustments, and Jeff and I agreed that we would further investigate our options. I was in no way, shape, or form ready to move forward on a plan that was half-baked at best. So I was ill-prepared for the mayhem I walked into that April day, just one week shy of my last day at work.

As I moved through the house, I noticed a fine layer of dust that seemed to hang in the air. Funny, the house was clean when

I left that morning. This was no ordinary dust. No no. This was a supremely special kind of dust, a dust that not only hung in the air, but also gracefully settled into crevices and nooks and crannies you didn't even know existed.

It slowly dawned on me that my sweet husband had started the remodel project *without telling me*. This fell into the category of "101 Things Brainless Men Do to Aggravate Their Wives." I searched desperately for the filter that usually occupied the space over my mouth and kept me from blurting out the first thing that came to my mind, but I couldn't find it. Instead I went straight for my husband, fire coming from eyes and smoke coming from my ears. "What in the world have you done?"

"What? We talked about this, remember?" He couldn't understand, even as he led me upstairs to look at the new tile in the upstairs bathrooms, why I would be upset.

Y'all, this dust—the remains of the pulverized old tile—was all over everything. Nothing had been spared. Nothing had been removed from the linen closets inside the very bathrooms where the destruction was taking place. Clean sheets, clean bath towels, clean hand towels, clean washrags were no longer clean. The first person to attempt to use one of those towels to dry off with would have only succeeded in creating a nice layer of mud all over their bodies.

Remember my office upstairs? Well, inside the closet of that room were the family scrapbooks. All my children's baby books, all the family albums, countless pictures that had yet to be placed into albums—every last one of them—were now covered in dust. Thick, nasty dust. And still Jeff was clueless. But that's okay. I took a deep breath and focused on my last week at work.

The house would have to wait.

· · ·

Marriage is a continual learning process. Having a wedding ring placed on your finger isn't the end of the game. We don't spike the ball and do our end-zone happy dance. Marriage is all about two different people trying to figure out how to live together in the same house without killing each other or the kids. Medaling for gold in a knockdown, drag-out, screamfest in front of the kids isn't the best option.

I think back to when Jeff and I were dating and then engaged. I never wanted to disagree with him because I was scared I'd run him off. I always tried to look my best for him. I wanted him to be happy with the choice he seemed to be making. We eloped to Maui, and I have to admit that just before our sunset ceremony on the beach, I was worried he would suddenly have a change of heart, change of mind—call it what you will—but the result would be me standing alone on a beach far from home with no husband.

Those fears were, of course, ridiculous.

Over the years, I've known many people who have forgotten the thrill of dating their spouses. Their wedding ceremony was the end of something instead of the beginning of something fabulous and exciting.

Jeff and I had been married for well over a decade by then, and we still had a wonderful time together. Even so, there were days when I didn't want to get out of my jammies (can I get an AMEN on that one?), and days would go by when shaving both legs just wasn't going to happen. But giving into those types of temptations too often, or for too long, will cause more problems than the pleasure a day of rest will provide.

A popular myth is floating around among young couples today that once you get married, you can just let everything hang out—and they do mean everything! Girls, I am here to tell you there is nothing sexy or attractive about being so comfortable around your spouse that you forget to put your best foot forward. Boys, this goes for you too. "Pull my finger" wasn't funny in fifth grade, and it is downright disrespectful as a married man.

The easiest "target" area of improvement involves staying in shape. As I mentioned, I was looking forward to going to the gym once I quit my job. I probably should include a little caveat here: I hate working out. I really do. I don't get any type of buzz or whatever those deranged, torture-loving folks get.

I exercise because it's good for me and also because it allows me to keep up with my extremely active kiddos. I like being able to launch a football farther than five feet for my boys. I like being able to pick up my kids and throw them across the pool. The benefits of exercise outweigh the irritations. Having said that, I'm also continually looking for new ways to work out with the least amount of effort.

That brings me to the Shake Weight.

I was watching TV one day, and this commercial came on introducing the latest and greatest in home fitness equipment: an amazing weight device for your arms. You shake this thing— hence the name—and a free-flowing weight inside moves back and forth at a rapid rate of more than two hundred times a minute. In just six minutes, you'll be on your way to supremely cut arms! No more flyaway, flappy wings that you try to shove into shirts or hide under sweaters. No, ma'am! With this miracle device for only $29.99, you too can be fit and trim for the summer!

Then they showed all these women with beautiful arms and shoulders. Can you believe that? Well, I did—hook, line, and sinker. From the looks of the Shake Weight in the commercial, the free-floating weight somehow moved by itself. Um—WRONG. You have to shake it. Brilliant. Yes, folks, my blond hair is real. And for good measure, this thing is heavy—that's where the "weight" part of the name comes into play. I bought it. I tried it. I discovered that six minutes is an eternity when you're holding an eight-pound weight at chest level and trying to shake it with one hand. What a letdown. I now use the Shake Weight as a new-agey, super-stylish doorstop.

Thankfully, I found another way of toning my arms—painting. This was the direct result of my husband's other exceptional idea (besides the bathroom demolition): the redistribution of space upstairs. We sat the kids down and told them we were moving my office downstairs and they would all be getting new rooms. Hooray!

The layout of the second floor is perfect for our family. Walk with me as we go on a little tour. As you reach the top of the stairs, to your right is a bedroom, which the boys shared, and another room directly in front of you, which belonged to Emma. Also at the top of the stairs is a miniature landing, sort of like a computer nook. This small space doubles as a catch-everything-that-doesn't-have-a-real-home space. Oh, and somewhere beneath the Lego magazines, *American Girl* magazines, and Junie B. Jones books, which miraculously could not be placed on the bookshelf three feet away, there lies a computer desk.

To the left of the nook is a bathroom and a bit farther left is the step up into the playroom. Across the playroom—watch your step—you find yourself in a hallway. To your right is my office and to the left is my sister's vacated room, the makeshift guest room. (She left all her bedroom furniture with us prior to her move to California, which worked out great for us. A complete bedroom suite wouldn't fit in the back seat of her Honda compact.) Between these two rooms is a "Jack and Jill" bathroom. It's this side of the house that hadn't been used well.

To correct that, the walls needed to be painted. Sounds easy, right? Not so much. The furniture had to be moved. Where to put it? Why, the playroom, of course.

Jeff and I decided that this would be a fun (ha!) project to do together. The kids would still be in school through the month of May, so no chance of little "helping" hands. We could maneuver through the rooms quickly and swiftly and get this over and done in the short side of a week. Clearly, I had been inhaling too much paint. When Jeff said "we," I thought that meant side by side, you help me and I help you, and together—while in the same room—we would get this done. Silly girl.

The words "we" and "together" only meant that we would be in the same house.

Awesome.

So this half of the "we" (which translated nicely to "I") moved furniture. This half of the "we" packed up books and moved them to the attic. This half of the "we" primed and painted. Emma was moving out of her Care Bears–laden bedroom and into her brothers' old room. She was unquestionably electrified at the mere thought. The hiccup? Her old room was the new guest room, and Care Bears—though cute and cuddly—didn't exactly scream elegant and adult.

The bears had to be painted over. I painted those Care Bears onto her wall years ago. My sister and I mixed the paint so it was exactly the right shade for each Bear (Bedtime Bear, Good Luck Bear, Funshine Bear, and more) and painstakingly, with loving care, put those bears on each wall. Now they were coming down. I could cry. Truth be told, I did cry.

But what really got to me was that it took two coats of primer to cover the stinking things! Up and down, back and forth. Who needs the Shake Weight? The Care Bears were effectively covered with primer, a stark contrast of white splotches up against the pale creamy yellow of the walls. I would fix that later when I returned with the paint. Next, I moved into Emma's new room and was greeted by a ten-foot-tall, eight-foot-wide tree mural on the boys' wall.

Again, two coats of primer, but as an added bonus with this room, I had to do the ceiling because the tree's canopy stretched up and over half of it. I began contemplating the top ten ways to inflict bodily harm on a person (let's say a husband, just for giggles), using a paint can and a paint roller as your only weapons. With every trip up and down the ladder, I would think that this was supposed to be *our* project. This was something we could do together. Being in the same house did not count as together! Inevitably, my mind would wander . . .

If I hit him with a full can of paint, will he figure out I'm not liking my new role as the hired help? Probably not. He'll probably think I just slipped. Slipped. There's a thought. Paint is slippery. If I pour it on the garage floor, and he happens to slip—nope, scratch that. If I pour paint on the garage floor . . . I'm the one who'll have to clean it up.

Up the ladder, lugging the roller, losing my balance, trying with unsuccessful grace to stop myself from getting tangled in the rungs, I let some very colorful words go flying. You'd think that would have been my breaking point. It wasn't.

My breaking point came two days later. I had just finished Emma's new room—from floor to ceiling. The mural was gone. I had actually finished something!

As moms, we rarely get to finish anything in a day's time. Laundry, for instance, is never finished. Honestly, I don't know what the bottom of my clothes hamper looks like—I don't think I have ever seen it. The kitchen? Is it ever really clean? I don't think so. As soon as you finish one meal, it's practically time to start the next one, or at the very least, someone wants a snack.

I was coming to terms with the "we" project turning into a "me" project with occasional supervision from Jeff (he had been hearing the crashes and colorful words as they filtered down the stairs and into his home office). I had been feeling guilty about abandoning my Shake Weight, and my gym had been sending little "We Miss You" cards, so this whole painting and moving furniture thing was working well for me.

After gathering my supplies, I moved to Emma's old room, which would eventually become the new guest room. I poured paint into the tray and set my shoulders (and my back) for the task of painting another room. It didn't take long to find my rhythm: dip, drip, roll; dip, drip, roll.

Enter husband.

Jeff looked around at my progress and said, "Wow. You're getting pretty good at this painting thing. Nice little workout, isn't it?"

I agreed with him on the workout part, but I was leery about his motives. What was he grinning about? (Dip, drip, roll.)

"The upstairs will look nice when we get everything moved around, don't you think?" He asked me as he fiddled with the edge of my paint tray.

"Uh-huh." (Dip, drip, roll.)

He cleared his throat. "Hey, I was thinking about having new windows installed upstairs, you know, since the upstairs is already torn apart. What do you think?"

I stopped in mid-roll. *What do I think?* My mind was having trouble processing the last thing he'd said. *New windows?*

Oh my stars!

Let me help you catch up to where I was in that moment: on the downhill slope of the upstairs switcheroo. Or so I thought. Having new windows installed just tacked on another two to three weeks of unrest in my house. I put my paint roller in its tray, sat down on the floor, leaned my back up against a freshly painted wall, and began to cry. I swear that tears to a man are like Kryptonite to Superman. My cool, confident, never-at-a-loss-for-words husband knelt down on the floor and gawked at me, speechless. He couldn't for the life of him figure out why I was so upset.

Remember what I said about how we need to always put our best foot forward—even after we get married? Especially after we get married?

Well, the remodeling project is the perfect analogy. I love my house. It fits our family. But it had a rundown look and feel. Jeff was doing to the house (and for me, I might add) what I was trying to do with the Shake Weight.

Having babies and raising kids will wear you out. As moms, we also get that worn-out look and feel. As mothers we have high-volume traffic areas just like our carpets. For me, my high-volume traffic area is the pooch I will most likely forever carry around my midsection—unless I enlist the help of a gifted surgeon. Y'all, having three babies in twenty-six months will stretch out your skin to the point that it looks and feels exactly like the area of carpet leading to your kitchen!

There really isn't anything I can do about it. Sit-ups are from the devil. The Roman chair at the gym is Satan's favorite torture tool, which women use to try to tighten skin that is happy to just hang. But I still try. I believe that not only am I charged with doing what I can to keep my body in good working order and condition so I can keep going, but I do it for my husband. He deserves to still be able to see the woman he fell in love with all those years ago. Even if seeing her means he catches only a glimpse of her through a veil of spit-up, diapers, and a blur of motion as she runs child A and child B to different practices.

I've worn my hair long for years. It's a style I always seem to go back to. I didn't choose this particular hairstyle because it makes me look absolutely fabulous, but because it's easy. A quick twist and a clip or a rubber band works wonders when time to blow-dry has vanished. Still, every so often I'll cut my hair. My poor hairdresser hates it when I get into moods like that. She will obediently cut off about seven or eight inches of long blond hair and turn what is left into a super-cute, spunky do.

I'm never able to duplicate the style she gives me, but it looks great while I'm in her chair! The first time Jeff sees me after one of these chop sessions, he goes completely bananas, not because he's upset that I cut off all my hair, but because he loves a short and sassy cut.

Short hair is ten times more of a pain in the backside to fix every day than long hair. Short hair requires a buffet of products to keep whichever style I managed to get it into that morning.

But do you know how much better I feel when my hair is fixed? For starters, it means I have probably taken a shower that day, and that's almost always a good place to start. When my kids were babies, it was very difficult to perform the seemingly menial daily tasks I used to take for granted: brushing my teeth before noon, showering, getting dressed. Once Jeff and I started having all the kids, I had to become deliberate about those daily tasks.

I want to encourage you to do something outrageous. I want to challenge you to let your baby cry while you hop into the shower and do a Ginsu shave on both legs today. Stick Junior in his crib or bring him into the bathroom with you, but the bottom line is this: take a shower. Then put on a little makeup, dry your hair, and get dressed. You don't have to dress to the nines, but just getting out of your jammies will do wonders for your mind. Your husband will think he has come home to the wrong house!

. . .

I've picked on us moms about our daily habits, but here's a tidbit for the dads. They make Shake Weights for men too! Have y'all looked at recent TV sitcoms? A double standard is being portrayed. I mean, we already discussed that TV and movies have lied to us about the way a pregnancy should go—why should parenting and marriage be any different?

I can think of a couple of different shows that show the wife/mother as svelte and smart and stunning. The husband/dad? He is a ginormous ignoramus. He is dumpy and overweight. He isn't very intelligent. He isn't the head of the family. He sets a slovenly example. Most men don't struggle with the daily shower thing, most likely because they have to get up and go to work every day. Think about it—what would happen if a man didn't shower or get dressed and then went into the office? He would most likely be fired.

Other areas of concern between a husband and wife are simply not present between a dating boyfriend and a girlfriend. Take bathroom etiquette, for example. I read an article in *Cosmo* many moons ago about things you should never let your man see you doing. I don't remember most of the top ten, but the one thing that jumped out at me was this: Never let your man see you brush your teeth. It isn't very graceful or elegant, but it is a highly necessary part of a bathroom routine.

Guys, take note. If witnessing us brushing our teeth is an off-limits area, what does that say about some of the bathroom stunts y'all pull? There needs to be respectful and healthy boundaries set around certain activities. For starters, close the bathroom door. Even though the husband is supposed to be the head of the house and the king of the castle—seeing him on his throne just doesn't scream, "I want you! Take me now!" Be respectful of your wife's feelings and perhaps her sense of smell.

I realize not everyone has the ability to join a fitness facility because of location or financial obligations, but the gym is not the only way to get some exercise. The babies who probably wreaked a great deal of havoc on your body are more than just cute and cuddly. They are bona fide and certified weights. You can lie on your back and lift your baby over your head and then put her back on your tummy. She will think you're playing with her, and your arms get a terrific workout.

Or you and your man can strap that baby in a stroller and strike out on foot together for a little evening walk around the neighborhood. This is a double bonus: You both get some exercise and quality communication time because Peanut is occupied taking in all the sights around her.

Being married with children really is about the same as living in a house you're remodeling. It is loud. It is messy. And something constantly needs your attention.

Now back to my own little remodel job. I had to control my tears and reassure my husband that I really wasn't crazy, but the chances were high that I'd arrive at that destination soon. I took a deep breath and reminded myself that I wasn't talking to a first-rate imbecile or even someone who was deliberately trying to drive me out of mind. I was talking to my husband, the man who loves me and who genuinely wants to do nice things for me. It's at times like these that we tend to speak different languages.

I agreed to the new windows. And then I agreed to the new carpet. He promised to help me put the house back together because our upstairs looked like we were auditioning for the TV series *Hoarders.* We had to climb over piles of stuff just to get from one side of the room to the other.

The windows were installed upstairs with very little mishap, the children adjusted to their new rooms, and Jeff and I both learned that a little communication goes a *long, long* way.

12.

The Wrestling Match

Several years ago for New Year's weekend, we hitched up Nelson and ventured out to one of the nearby state parks for some rest and relaxation, Texas-style. In short, we went camping. One of our close friends wanted to go too, so both families made the road trip up Interstate Highway 45. The winters in southeast Texas are mild and most of the time beautiful. They make living here in the summer bearable. We don't typically get hit with the blistering cold that the rest of the country is hammered with until February, and even then, our winter only lasts a week or two.

The family we went with, the McCoys, have two girls close in age to our kids, who were seven, eight, and nine then. We both had campers, a bicycle for each family member, and chairs to sit in 'round the campfire. And thanks to Big Mac's new Christmas iPod, we had a seemingly endless supply of old-time country and western music. We were set up to have a fun four days.

The Lake Livingston State Park is gorgeous. I believe that no other place in the country grows pine trees quite like east Texas. They're tall and sturdy and mighty. Throughout the park, there are beautiful hiking and biking trails.

I learned to ride a bike when I was very young. But it had been too many years to count since I braved that two-wheel mode of transportation, so as excited as my children were to scoot around pine trees and rocks and jump curbs as if they were training to be the next extreme bicyclists, I was more cautious. The McCoys were also much better on their bikes than I was.

One afternoon, after we had been there for a couple of days, the kids wanted to go for a bike ride. I could see the mischievous look in Ethan's eyes—he was seriously thinking about some major daredevil stunts. So I was seriously thinking about letting the dads do this one alone.

But my sweet husband had other ideas. He reached around behind me and hollered to the McCoys, "Hey, y'all mind taking our kids for a bit?" Jeff was grinning from ear to ear like the Cheshire Cat from *Alice in Wonderland*. He gave Big Mac a guys-only wink-wink just in time for our daughter Emma to see it.

As if having a "locker room discussion" right in front of me weren't bad enough, Emma looked at her daddy and at me, and then turned to the McCoys and said, "Oh, they're probably just gonna wrestle. They wrestle a lot."

Big Mac and Lesli almost fell off their bikes.

Honestly if Jeff hadn't been holding me up, I probably would have slid to the ground and under the closest rock. Big Mac was crying he was laughing so hard, and Lesli was laughing and blushing. Big Mac had to ask, "So Emma, Mommy and Daddy wrestle, huh?"

"Yep."

"Who wins?"

Emma smiled and rode her bike in a circle, not knowing the agony she was causing her mother or the satisfaction she was giving her father. "Oh, Mommy wins. All the time."

Choke.

Okay, this brings us to a very intricate, vital part of life for a married couple with kids. Sex. We can't survive this parenting thing without a little hand-to-hand communication with our spouses. I know you know how to do this. I mean, you had kids—even if you adopted your precious little ones, the act of *trying* was still involved.

Life with kids is hard. Let's face it, when you have been spit-up on, thrown-up on (yes, there is a difference), done twenty-seven loads of laundry and you still can't see the bottom of the hamper, made three complete meals and numerous snacks, having some quality couch time with your honey probably isn't ranking very high for a couple of reasons. One, you're flat-out exhausted, and having sex takes some energy. And two, Baby Vomit #5 isn't the most appealing perfume on the market, so you may not be feeling particularly sexy.

I received an email in my inbox a while ago that speaks to this very predicament. Allow me to paraphrase:

Housework is typically seen as a woman's job, but one evening Fran arrived home from work to find that the kids had been bathed, one load of laundry was in the washer, and another one was in the dryer. Dinner was on the stove and smelled delicious, and the table had been set. Fran was amazed!

It turns out that Fran's husband, Fred, had read an article that said wives who work full-time and had to do their housework were too tired to have sex.

The night went great, and the next day she told her office friends all about it:

"We had a wonderful dinner. Fred even cleaned the kitchen. He helped the kids with their homework, folded all of the laundry, and put it away. I really enjoyed my evening."

*"But what happened afterward?" her friends wanted
to know.*

Fran giggled, "Oh that. Fred was too tired."

Go ahead and laugh, but this is all true. In the previous chapter,
I talked about the necessity of maintaining your physical health.
Now I want to talk about the extreme importance of maintaining a healthy sex drive after the kids make their appearance. In
the beginning of most relationships, we don't sit down and make
a list of the jobs or roles we'll each play. For instance, after Jeff
and I got married, we didn't take a pad and a pencil and write
down who does what—with "always initiating sex" falling into
his column. Nowhere does it say that the initiator must always
be your husband. In fact, to keep things lively, go to him before
he has a chance to come to you. Folks, sex is a gift to be shared
and enjoyed.

This area of marriage and parenting has so many stumbling
blocks that will trip up couples. Children are the most obvious
obstacles. The sheer time they require of their parents makes it
almost impossible to conform to the traditional timetables and
locations. I'm not about to get X-rated on you, but we're going to
talk about some things that will make some people uncomfortable.

It still amazes me that Jeff and I were able to have as many
kids as we did in such a short time. Just when I would get one
kid to sleep through the night, I would deliver a new one. I had
someone touching me all day long. I was always holding one who
just wanted "up" or I was nursing one because it was time or I
was pregnant with one, so touching any part of me could, at any
time, result in projectile vomiting.

When Jeff would come home and try to be frisky or loving or
want a little attention for himself, oftentimes I was the problem.
I didn't want another person touching me. My body wasn't my

own. I was an incubator or a cow—an automatic milk dispenser. On the occasion I was in the mood when he was in the mood, my body would present another issue. Did you know that the same hormone that releases a mother's milk is the same hormone she produces during sex? Kind of weird, but true.

Many nursing mothers have the ability to feed half the neighborhood until her milk is fully regulated, and that can take a long, long time, so whenever Jeff wanted to "wrestle," he would often get more than he bargained for. For the longest time, all I could picture was the milk ads from magazines: "Got Milk?" Why yes, yes I do! The automatic response of my body to let down the milk had sort of a drowning effect on the mood—literally. We had to learn to work around it.

Men and women view sex differently. The late author and speaker Gary Smalley once compared women to Crock-Pots and men to microwaves when it came to their readiness in the bedroom. Truer words have never been spoken. Girls, I don't have a magic "on" switch. A Crock-Pot takes time to warm up, whereas a microwave heats up instantly.

At the mere mention of sex, most men are raring and ready to go. With women, that isn't always the case. I can't "rev up" at the drop of a hat, especially after holding babies, feeding babies, and changing diapers all day. I need time to warm up to the idea. But when you're dealing with little bitty ones, time is a commodity you don't often have much of. I have said over and over again that we have to be intentional and deliberate in our parenting. We do. There's no way around that.

But we also have to be exceptionally deliberate and intentional when it comes to relations with our spouse. It's easy to get so caught up and derailed in the details of daily life that we forget about each other.

Please do not let this happen to your marriage.

. . .

I have particularly fond memories of my grandparents. Both are gone now, but as a kid, I spent a great deal of time with them. There wasn't any other place I would rather be than at their house. Mimi and Papa were married for over fifty years before they passed away.

One of my earliest memories of the two of them is from a Memorial Day trip to Lake Buchanan. Every year, my entire family (and I do mean entire—Mimi and Papa, aunts, uncles, cousins, parents, my sisters, and I) would travel about an hour and half north of Austin to the lake. We stayed in these little old cabins right on the water. We would rent two of them (think of a duplex), each of which had one room and two double beds, one bathroom, and a little kitchenette. Our really cool aunt and uncle, together with all eight of us grandkids, would hunker down in one cabin while the rest of the grown-ups stayed in the other.

I remember walking into the grown-up cabin one morning and seeing my grandparents still sleeping on their air mattress. They were snuggled so close together that at first glance I thought it was only one person lying there. That's how they did things. They did it together or not at all. Well into their sixties, they still chased each other with the fervor and vigor of a newlywed couple.

From the moment I saw them sleeping on the air mattress, I knew I wanted that. I wasn't going to settle for anything less. They were married in the 1940s. They saw war. They survived poverty. They had too many mouths to feed and not enough money to go around. Yet their love, their hunger for each other, remained strong. They were deliberate. It probably didn't hurt that they were both stubborn and strong-willed Germans!

I carried that memory, and all the others I collected throughout my years with them, into my marriage with Jeff. I knew what we could be if only we went after it. Marriage is hard, but with kids, it's almost impossible—unless you're willing to stand your ground and fight for what you have.

How do we do that?

Believe it or not, your family life shouldn't revolve around your children. How many folks did I upset by that statement? You and your husband should be the center of each other's eyes. I am not in any way, shape, or form telling you to ignore your children, but I am telling you to be careful about how much emphasis you place on them. There have been many times when I looked at Jeff, as sweet and wonderful as he is, and wanted to throw something hard and heavy at him (like a paint can, for instance). I am sure he would tell you the same thing about me. But it is precisely that passion, that spunk, and that sheer grit and determination that make us ache for each other when we're apart.

Eventually our kids (your kids) will grow up and leave home. That's the goal of proper parenting. You love these babies, you teach them, but in the end, they move out. What will be left is an empty house and a husband and a wife. The burning question is this: Will that husband and wife have any idea who the other one is? If you have spent the last twenty years putting your kids first in everything and placing them above your spouse, the answer is no, you will not.

We can't let that happen.

There is a great deal of emphasis today on the family bed, the practice of babies and children sleeping in the same bed as their parents. This is a crock! The family bed will quickly move from "family" to "Junior and Mom" while Dad retreats to Junior's abandoned bedroom.

In our house, the children's bedrooms are all upstairs and the master bedroom is downstairs through the living room. In short, we are far from our kids. Now that they are older, this isn't such a big deal, but it was when they were newborns and infants. We had a cradle in our room so the new babies could be close to me for the first weeks. This was practical—they were up every couple of hours. Also, getting up with one crying baby was difficult, but having that baby wake up another child would have been more than I could handle!

Once our babies started rolling around, it was time for them to be introduced to their new room. This was when I started writing names on all the baby monitors I kept beside my side of the bed. Jeff and I were on the same page from the get-go. We didn't want a child lying in between us at night. This wasn't about sex. We wanted—no, check that—we needed to be able to reach over and simply touch each other. Life was challenging enough without purposefully adding obstacles to separate us.

We learn by what we see. Sure, we can tell our children all day long until we're blue in the face what they need to do or how they should act, but the fact is they learn best by what they see and experience. Here's a good example: my grandparents and me. They never sat me down and told me the secret to a long, successful, and happy marriage. I picked that up from watching them. What kind of message are you sending to your kids if you let them get in between you and your husband every single night?

There are exceptions to every rule. I'm not a monster. Kids get sick and they need to be beside you. They have bad dreams that will not go away by turning on a light—they need to be comforted by the touch that only comes from Mom or Dad. I get that.

Kids also need boundaries. They need to be taught and shown how to respect your boundaries as parents. Our children aren't invited to cross the lines associated with the marital bed, and the lock on the bedroom door reinforces our words.

Let me give you examples. I have some friends who have been married for fifteen or so years. They have two children: a boy thirteen and a girl almost ten. To this very day, neither child sleeps in his or her own bed. Their daughter sacks out in her parents' bed right between Mom and Dad. And their son? Well, he is around the corner on the couch in the living room. Their lives revolve around their kids. Granted, they are some of the most involved parents I have ever known. She volunteers for everything under the sun at both of her children's schools. He coaches everything from baseball to soccer to gymnastics. But what about them as a couple? That's a completely different story.

Now, let's look at the opposite side of that spectrum.

I'm going to get letters because of this chapter. I can feel it.

Ethan was introduced to his first babysitter when he was six weeks old. I "borrowed" her from the nursery at church. I knew her and her family. She had helped me over that summer as I taught (in a very pregnant state) Vacation Bible School. I felt comfortable leaving our son with her. It was the first time Jeff and I had gone out to eat since he was born.

I worried about Ethan throughout the entire meal. I called four times in an hour and a half. When we arrived back home and found him asleep in her arms, the house still standing and no visible signs of fire damage, we hired her again two weeks later.

The next time she came over, Jeff and I went out for dinner and saw a movie. I called once. Jeff and I began to enjoy each other as a couple. Obviously we were enjoying ourselves because soon after I got pregnant with Emma! It's imperative that you maintain your identity as husband and wife as well as playing the role of mom and dad. Your family will suffer into the next generation if you fail in this area. But no pressure.

Something else Jeff and I have done: take mini-vacations without the kids. I know that statement right there will cause some of you reading this book to hunt me down, but hear me out. I'd like to ask you a question. I want you to think about this before you answer. Do you like your spouse? I'm almost certain you love your spouse, but do you *like* your spouse? Can you imagine yourself going away for a weekend with just him? No kids, no friends, only the two of you. Would you have anything to talk about other than the kids? What would you do? Where would you go?

When Jeff has to go somewhere for a couple of days on business, I'll often go with him. We will ask his mother to come over and watch the kids or call one of our sitters to come in and help out so the two of us can have some alone time together. It's wonderful—marvelous. I don't have all the adjectives to describe it. We are able to reconnect on levels that are amazingly refreshing for our bodies and our spirits.

We live just outside Houston, and when the kids were little, we had the opportunity to spend one night in one of the super-fancy downtown hotels. Y'all, we totally jumped on that! It was for only one night just down the road from home, but we had so much fun together, it might as well have been the other side of the world! You may be wondering, *But what about the kids? What will they feel like when Mom and Dad leave? Will they feel abandoned? Rejected?*

No, no, and no.

The kids will be fine. Most kids love hanging out with new people, especially if they have been exposed to them from early on. The date nights, dinners, and little overnight getaways are warm-up exercises for the marathon of an actual, out-of-town, long haul, Mom-and-Dad-only vacation. Throughout the years, Jeff and I have been blessed with the resources to go away for some nice vacations alone. The time we spent together has been priceless.

When the kids were one, two, and three, we went to Italy for two and a half weeks. My heart aches to go back there. We left the kids with three different rotations of grandparents while we were gone. I'm not sure who had more fun—the kids, the grand-parents, or us! I realize that Italy is one of those once-in-a-lifetime dream destinations. I get that. Aside from the sights we saw and the places we visited, Jeff and I were in a foreign country where we had to rely on each other. Neither one of us speaks Italian, although we figured out *vino* (wine) quickly. Wow, the memories we made together—and the wrestling matches we scored!

Those getaways are only a taste of what will come after the kids leave home, but none of that will be possible if we don't keep in touch with each other in the interim.

I have the privilege of speaking to a lot of moms' groups, and one of the saddest things I hear from women is a lack of respect both for their husbands and from their husbands. Intimacy is not merely a physical act. Intimacy is very personal—intact intimacy affects your very spirit. If you have wounded your spouse's heart, how difficult will it be to touch your spouse's body? How difficult will it be for your spouse to touch yours?

So many couples today are dealing with respect issues that it just breaks my heart. Respect is a two-way street. Jeff and I are trying (some days are better than others) to teach our boys that girls go first. Is it always fair? No. But sometimes life isn't fair, and girls should still go first. Girls are special above all else in creation and they need to be treated accordingly. Even sisters.

Respect, or rather *disrespect*, between a husband and a wife takes on a myriad of different faces.

Many of the groups I speak to are MOPS groups (Mothers of Pre-Schoolers, mops.org). This is a fabulous organization that affirms and builds up the mothers of children ages kindergarten and younger. The women are divided into small discussion groups, and the talk inevitably turns to husbands. The banter that goes back and forth between these women makes me wonder why they got married in the first place:

"My husband never gets up with the baby . . . never helps with the kids . . . never picks up his clothes . . . always plays golf on the weekends . . . never defends me to his mother . . . always makes fun of my cooking . . ."

Then there is my personal favorite, when the conversation turns to sex: "I'm not giving him any until he learns to help me with the kids!" Ouch. Y'all, our men aren't five-year-olds who need to be given a time-out. Sex isn't a tool or, worse, a *weapon*. Sex is a gift. The only way to realize that is to see our spouses the way we used to, which means looking at them through pre-baby goggles.

Ladies, our husbands aren't big, stupid lumps. They have a purpose and a plan. They have feelings. It's just that we really do speak different languages. We were each designed and created to complement each other, like puzzle pieces. Sometimes we will be like polar opposites, but in the end, we should always come back together.

Can I challenge you to take some action? When you find yourself in the middle of a husband-bashing session, will you stop, take a breath, and try to say something edifying about your spouse? One kind word has the power to redirect an entire conversation gone amuck.

Sounds easy, right? What if you're really miffed at your man? I just happen to have a story to illustrate my point.

A while back, Jeff had to go out of town for business to San Antonio, about a three-hour drive from Houston. It was a last-minute kind of thing that I thought he could have gotten out of if he'd really wanted to. He went ahead and made his plans to go, leaving behind one supremely annoyed wife. One day into his trip, he called and asked me to join him. We could walk on the River Walk, tour the Alamo, and do all the goofy things tourists do. Oh, and we could celebrate my birthday.

I told him exactly where he could put the Alamo. I had already been there, and if he was so keen on seeing the River Walk, maybe he could jump in and go for a little swim. I wasn't having it. I hung up.

I was fairly pleased with myself. Just like riding a bicycle is something you don't quickly forget, spitting fire is something that also returns to you in the blink of an eye. My stunned husband didn't call back. I, on the other hand, picked up the phone and called a friend for a congratulatory conversation about what a bonehead I was married to.

The girlfriend I called has been my friend since we were eighteen. She knows me better than I know myself. She has seen me at my best and at my absolute worst. Somehow, through all of that, she still loves me. Naturally, she would be the one I called. I relayed the conversation to her, feeling quite proud of the way I handled the situation. I was totally unprepared for her response.

"Are you out of your mind?" she asked once I stopped long enough to take a breath.

"Excuse me?"

"Why would you say those things to him? D, he loves you. He provides for you—"

"Yeah, but he went out of town for my birthday, as if I wasn't important."

"And that gives you the right to one hundred percent disrespect him to him and then to me? You need to be on your knees thanking God He gave you this man. You could be without a husband."

That cut right through me. I was instantly sorry. She doesn't have a husband. She doesn't have the gift I have. She saw something so clearly, so unmistakably plainly, that when she pointed it out to me, her voice quivered with anger. I expected the anger, though not directed at me.

I immediately called my husband back and told him I'd be in San Antonio the next morning. I apologized to him for the things I had said and for the things I had said about him.

Y'all, it's crucial that we build up our spouses. Just about every aspect of society will do its level best to tear them down. It is up to us to protect them.

As our kids got older, we had to come up with more evasive terminology for what actually went on behind the closed and locked door of our bedroom. We told them we were "talking."

But the more I thought about this, the more I liked "wrestling."

After that New Year's weekend with the McCoys, the word took on a whole new meaning. I'd like to share some of the things I learned, and you can determine for yourself if "wrestling" is the right word for the horizontal dance between husband and wife. You might be surprised. The *Merriam-Webster* online dictionary defines "wrestling" as "a sport or contest in which two unarmed individuals struggle hand to hand with each attempting to subdue or unbalance the other." How's that for accurate?

Have you ever been knocked off-balance by your man? I have. It's awesome. During this whole let's-flip-the-house-on-its-side-and-turn-it-inside-out adventure, I had the opportunity to watch Jeff take some things apart and put them back together. He focuses so intently on whatever task he's working on that it truly takes my breath away and makes my knees go weak. In short, I am completely knocked off-balance.

I watched him take down a ceiling fan in one room and switch it with another one in a different room. I was mesmerized just watching him, and now even thinking about it, I smile. Do you have a moment like that you can draw from? Somewhere between the diapers, the dinners, and the ball games, can you pull out a memory of your man and travel back in time and let that memory push your button?

If you don't, put the kids to bed early tonight and call your mother-in-law to watch them or put in a movie for them upstairs and get busy making that memory today! Be intentional about your spouse. In this world of technology in a millisecond, let him know you're thinking about him. Shoot him a spicy text message at three o'clock in the afternoon. Chances are, he won't dawdle on the way home from work. Do you remember those long good-night kisses you used to share before you got married? Try sending him off to work with that to think about. Rev his engine first thing in the day. Then keep it on a slow hum all day long.

We don't have to spend three weeks in Italy drinking red wine, eating cheese, and making love in foreign hotel rooms to recreate the lost romance in our child-ridden marriages. We have all the tools we need right here at home. All we need is imagination, some pre-planning, and an open and willing heart.

Try looking at each other as Man and Woman, instead of just Mom and Dad. If you take the bull by the horns every once in a while, the rewards will be awesome.

Girls, think about all the energy and attention we put into our babies. If we spent a third of that energy on our men, I guarantee you the divorce rate in this country would go down. It's time we take our families back! That starts with our marriages. If you were to ask any one of my children if they felt loved, adored, and treasured by their parents, they would look at you like you were nuts and answer, "Of course." But if you ask them, when it comes to Dad, who comes first, you or Mom? Hands down, their answer would be "Mom!"

Our children know they are loved. We tell them. We hug on them. We kiss them. We take care of them. But the number one way they know they are loved is by the way Mom and Dad love each other. Jeff and I have provided—are providing—them with the foundation of trust and solidarity to last them a lifetime. This is how life is supposed to work. This is how husbands are supposed to treat their wives. This is how wives are supposed to treat their husbands. We are a team. And we are just getting started.

Epilogue: Squirrel!

Early on, my husband and I decided that to make things easier on us, we would have the same set of house rules for all our kids. That seemed to be the logical way to do this rather than having different rules for each kid.

Several years ago, when my kids were much younger, I had one of those days. I was walking through the upstairs to return a Nintendo DS to its proper resting place when I came across a root beer can. An empty root beer can. It was in an odd place. Soft drinks don't live upstairs—they don't even get to visit there, especially since the new carpet arrived. Any accomplice of these visiting soft drinks would have some medieval-type punishments brought down upon them.

As it was, I picked up the lone root beer can and continued my journey to return the stranded DS. I had made it only a couple of feet when I noticed a pile of clothes sticking out from under the couch in the playroom. Clothes don't typically live under the couch. I put the root beer can and the DS on the side table and bent down to collect the lost clothes. I found socks, undies of varying owners, a bathing suit, and a pair of pajama bottoms.

While on my hands and knees, I also came across scissors that are supposed to reside in the kitchen.

I stood up, put the scissors in my back pocket, scooped up the clothes, nabbed the root beer can and the DS, and headed to Emma's bathroom where the laundry chute is located. To open the linen closet door, I had to set the root beer can down on the counter, where it instantly stuck like glue to the gobs of Crest for Kids toothpaste. I groaned, switched the DS to the other hand, opened the door, and attempted to drop the clothes down the laundry chute. No dice. The laundry chute was blocked.

Yes, it's true that I typically wait until Emma is forced into Spider Man underwear to do laundry, but no way was the chute that full. I began to pull items out one at a time. Towel after towel, sheet after sheet, then jeans and a board game (not sure what they were trying to prove with that!), another towel, the spare comforter from the guest room (come to find out, that's where the majority of the root beer went—I made a mental note to check the bed for remnants of more root beer).

Eventually clothes started tumbling down the chute, and I could hear the happy sounds of them hitting the hamper below. I also heard the conspicuous sounds of Lego pieces plinking against the sides. I returned my attention to the lost pile of clothes that had started this scavenger hunt of sorts and the abandoned DS from some thirty minutes earlier. Into the chute went the clothes, down the ramp (now unobstructed), and into the hamper. I turned to pick up my companion—the DS—and reached for the root beer can but found it cemented to the counter. I needed supplies to unstick it.

Still holding the DS in my hand, I went downstairs to the kitchen, set the DS on the counter, opened the cabinet under the sink, and retrieved the necessary supplies for unsticking the root beer can. Back upstairs I went. After another thirty minutes in

Emma's bathroom, I decided that since I was already up there with all my supplies, it made good sense to attack the boys' bathroom as well. Forty-five minutes later, the job was completed. But on my way through Ethan's room, I detected the unmistakable aroma of corn nuts. I felt like a bloodhound as I sniffed in and around the nooks and crannies of his room trying to locate the source of the smell.

Bingo! Jackpot! Evidently, Ethan had gotten hungry one night and had gone downstairs to snag a bag of corn nuts, and then proceeded to eat them in his bed.

Gross was the first thing that came to my mind. Ethan sleeps on the top bunk of a set of bunk beds. Terrific.

Naturally, I had to change the sheets. When I pulled the fitted sheet from the mattress, corn nuts flew through the air. Happy thoughts of what I was going to do to my firstborn after school filled my mind. I put clean sheets on his bed, picked up all the corn nuts from the floor, gathered my cleaning supplies, and began making my way to the stairs. I was halfway across the playroom when OUCH!

Lego sets are the bane of my existence. I never step on them when I'm wearing shoes. I find every single spare part when I'm barefooted. It is totally amazing.

I dropped the sheets, put down the cleaning supplies, and began picking up the pieces and depositing them into their home-base tub. Then I bent down to gather sheets and supplies, got all the way down the stairs and into the laundry room, started the sheets in the washer, and began the return trip through the living room to the kitchen. Pause. I saw the Sunday paper. There are coupons in the Sunday paper. I did need to make a run to the grocery store. Truth be told, I always need to make a trip to the store.

Plopping down on the floor, I thumbed through the ad section and spotted a few good coupons. I got up to get some scissors and remembered seeing some in the playroom, so I returned upstairs and began searching for them. They weren't in the play-room, but I did find a lovely collection of naked Barbie dolls that belonged in Emma's room. I gathered those and headed toward my daughter's room. I was thinking maybe she had scissors. She always has stuff like that.

So I put away the Barbies and looked for the scissors. I couldn't find them, but I did find a glue bottle that had been knocked over. I began to visualize what I would do to Emma once she came home from school.

I went back downstairs to get the necessary equipment to re-move the glue from the inside of a drawer. I realized that what I needed for the job should be in my bathroom. On my way through my bedroom, I saw that I forgot to make my bed. I stopped to make the bed, pick up the spare socks Jeff had left on the floor on his side of the bed, and carry them to the laundry basket in our closet. Perfect! The basket was full.

I sat down and began to sort clothes. I heard the bell on the washer, letting me know that Ethan's sheets were ready for the dryer. So I grabbed a load of whites and went to the laundry room. After transferring one load from the washer to the dryer, I started another load in the washer.

Then I returned to the kitchen area for a time check. I would have to leave soon to get the kids from school. I saw the dogs' food bowl was empty, so I went to the garage to fill the bowl and take it back to the kitchen, where I saw the DS from that morn-ing that never got put away in the first place!

I picked it up, determined this time to put it where it belonged, and headed back upstairs. As I rounded the corner at the top of the stairs, from the corner of my eye, I saw the contraband root beer can still sitting on my now-clean bathroom counter.

Had I completely lost my mind?

When I reached for the can, I half expected it to move away from me. I was thankful it didn't and continued my journey to put away the DS.

Mission accomplished. With the DS now securely in Elliott's room and the root beer can in hand, I went down the stairs. Seeing the newspaper on the living room floor, I walked over to the paper, set down the root beer can, glanced up at the clock, and ran out the door to grab the kids from school.

As all four of us walked into the door of the house, Ethan reached into my back pocket, pulled out the scissors I had put in my pocket for safekeeping six hours earlier, and handed them to me.

Emma picked up the root beer can and threw it away.

And Elliott folded up the paper and carried it to Jeff's office.

Have you ever had one of those days?

With kids, we have those days a lot. I feel as though I don't ever really get anything done, but I have a lot of practice walking in circles.

That reminds me of the Disney movie *Up* we used to watch several years ago. I'm fond of kid movies that offer adult humor for Mom and Dad, little added bonuses like that make the whole, let's-watch-this-movie-again-and-again-and-again-and-again thing, well, tolerable. At the end of the movie, the talking dogs are chasing Doug (the other talking dog) via airplanes. The dogs are flying around and around and they're closing in on our hero.

Then all of a sudden, Russell (the kid in the movie) yells out, "Squirrel!"

The dogs crash into one another as they each look for the prized squirrel. They took their eyes off our hero for an instant and all was lost. In a dog's world, squirrels represent the end-all, be-all of walking, talking squeaky toys. Dogs love them. They can't get enough of them. They can almost never catch them, but that doesn't stop them from trying. A squirrel can derail even the most trained and obedient dog.

Like the dogs, I chase my own "squirrels." It took me all day to get the root beer can and the DS in their rightful places—and even then, my kids had to help out!

During my time with you, I have shared my thoughts on how to raise happy, healthy kids who will one day grow into balanced, productive members of society. My way of doing things isn't the only way, but it's working for Jeff and me.

When the kids were babies and I'd take them out in public, people would ask me, "How do you do it?"

I have an excellent circle of friends. I have never tried to do this parenting thing alone.

At times, it is dangerous and should *not* be attempted alone. If you're a single parent, my heart goes out to you on another level entirely. You have no one to tag-team with—you are always IT. But that doesn't mean you are necessarily alone. In almost every city across this nation, you can find moms groups of some sort. The women in these groups are struggling with the same issues you are. Get connected with one. Find a church. I met some of my very best friends at church.

When Jeff and I started having all these babies, I was stuck in my house with no family nearby to help me. That was an excellent recipe for disaster. Then my neighbor dragged me to a MOPS meeting. I cannot stress the importance of friendship enough. You will need friends. Your husband will need friends. There will be days when your house looks like you test nuclear warheads in the living room. That's okay. I promise you there is another mom down the street whose house can match yours.

Epilogue: Squirrel!

Our kiddos are only small for a time, even though it seems like that time will never end. Not only will having a good and solid circle of friends save your sanity, but they will also help you find the strength you didn't know you had. They are like your own personal cheerleaders when you don't think you can put one more foot in front of the other. Parenting is not for the faint of heart. Only the strong survive. But you can do this.

When the kids were babies (think zero, one, and two), a sweet older lady from church told me, "Dallas, the days are long—but the years go by fast." I rolled my eyes and continued my day, struggling along in survival mode. Looking back over the pages in this book, I can't help but smile at the fact that she was right.

It's been over twenty years since I saw two pink lines on my first pregnancy test. Twenty years. I vividly remember the sleepless nights and the tantrums—both from the kids and from me. I remember the school projects, the track meets, the baseball games, the graduations from kindergarten to first grade—and then from middle to high school.

Some days were very, very long. But I blinked, and the years were gone.

Over the past two decades, I watched the World Trade Center come down, dictators being overthrown, royal weddings, and celebrity scandals of every shape and size. I brought life into this world and watched it slip away, as we said goodbye to family members, friends, and pets. I taught our children to talk (then wished I'd waited longer on that skill), and I taught them to count, read, and drive. I rejoiced as they outgrew weird childhood diseases, only to be hit with a worldwide pandemic as they barely crossed the threshold into adulthood. My world and theirs is constantly changing. The one unshakable truth is nothing stays the same.

I have thoroughly enjoyed parenting my kids and being a wife. I'm even more excited about the stage that is coming next: grand-babies! Don't get too excited or too far ahead—we're not quite there yet. I am, however, entering the empty-nester phase of life. I've got all three kiddos securely settled at Texas A&M University, one nuclear engineering major, one education major, and the youngest bringing up the rear in business. Jeff and I plan to move out of the bustling metropolis of Houston, opting for some acreage a little further north so we can be closer to the kids.

Still, reminiscing though the early years makes me break out into a cold sweat and ask myself, *How did I do it*? Laughter. Luck. Love. And prayer. My stubborn streak probably helped too.

This life thing is hard. Parenting is hard. But you can do it.

Good luck—and have fun!

Acknowledgments

Jeff Louis: For two decades you have stood beside me and encouraged me. You have stood in front of me and protected me from threats—both real and imagined. You slew all the dragons I brought into our marriage from my past and those I came across in the present. You have stood behind me, urging me onward when I didn't think I had the strength, aptitude, or ability. You are my husband, the father of my children, and my best friend. I could not have written this book without you.

Ethan, Emma, and Elliott: Through the years, y'all have shown me what the inside of my heart looks like. You each taught me how to be better a person by allowing me to bumble my way through being your mother. I love each of you to the moon and back—and then back again.

My parents, Jonathan and Lucretia: I raised my kids based on what I saw, felt, and learned growing up in your home. Thank you for teaching me life lessons strong enough to stick and valuable enough to pass down through the generations. I love you both.

My sisters (Danielle, Natasha, and Kristina): If not for y'all, I wouldn't have been nearly as skilled at changing diapers as I was when my own children were born. Thank you for letting me practice my mothering skills on you.

Mike and Terri: Hopefully I didn't embarrass y'all too much. Living next door to the two of you during some of the most trying times of my parenting journey truly did save my sanity. I am so thankful God put you both in the middle of my family circus.

David and Lesli: Our family and our adventures wouldn't have been the same without y'all! You have loved my children as your own, cared for them when they were sick or scared, and disciplined them when they needed correction. You have shown me what true friendship looks like.

Christianne Debysingh: You joined my team in the eleventh hour and saved the day. Thank you for working hard and tirelessly to help this book succeed and me as well. I am grateful. What a blessing!

Sandra Jonas: Last, but definitely not least. My amazing editor and publisher—you had to learn a foreign language just to keep up with all the Texas slang and twang nestled within the pages of this book! I'm happy to announce you are now fluent in redneck. What a ride the past couple of years have been. Your steadiness, patience, and extreme attentiveness to detail have meant the world to me. You believed in this project, even when I was losing faith. You have been the voice of reason and calm. You cleaned everything up without losing me or my voice in the process. I'm grateful for your long hours and hard work. But most of all, I'm grateful to have met you. Your kind and gentle spirit is a rarity in today's world.

Photo Album

Our sunset wedding
ceremony in Maui,
Hawaii.

Ethan needs some
mommy time. I'm
pregnant with Elliott.

My grandparents.

Clockwise from left: Jeff and the kids; Granny (my mom) and Emma; and Nana (my mother-in-law) and the kids.

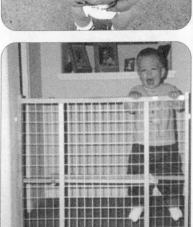

Clockwise from left: Unhappy campers Ethan (in time-out), Elliott, and Emma.

I dressed the kids in Texas Longhorn gear throughout their childhood, only to have them turn on me and become Texas Aggies!

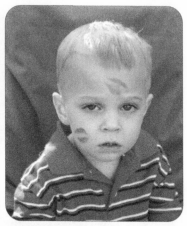

Disney World: Elliott with Cinderella (*left*) and after leaving the princess tent (*right*).

Emma's famous swan dive down the staircase at my brother-in-law's wedding.

Classy trio.

About the Author

DALLAS LOUIS grew up in Austin, Texas. She earned a BA degree in Christianity from Houston Baptist University and served as the women's ministry director of her church for seven years. A former field leader for MOPS (Mothers of Preschoolers) International, Dallas now travels the country speaking to women's groups, encouraging them in their faith, parenting, marriages, and ministries. Her first book, *Girlfriends, Giggles, and God,* is a thirty-one-day, humor-filled devotional, reflecting upon circumstances that arise in every woman's household. She lives in Houston with her husband and three children. Visit her online:

Website: dallaslouis.com
Facebook: @dallaslouisauthor
Instagram: @dhlouis
Twitter: @dallaslouis

Made in the USA
Coppell, TX
18 October 2024

38883299R00121